THE ANSWER TO THE CULT EXPLOSION

A PRACTICAL GUIDE TO ENABLE ANYONE TO
REFUTE THE FALSE TEACHINGS OF MOST
CULTIC AND DANGEROUS RELIGIOUS
GROUPS

FRED GRIGG, D.D., BR.ED

MANDATE MINISTRIES
GOLD COAST, AUSTRALIA

COPYRIGHT © 2014 F.R.GRIGG

All rights reserved. No part of this publication may be reproduced, distributed or transmitted in any form or by any means, including photocopying, recording, or other electronic or mechanical methods, without the prior written permission of the publisher, except in the case of brief quotations embodied in critical reviews and certain other noncommercial uses permitted by copyright law. For permission requests, write to:

Mandate Ministries Pty Ltd
Post Office Box 1457
Elanora, QLD, 4221 Australia

Website: http://mandateministries.com.au

The Answer to the Cult Explosion – 7th Edition Revised

Cover by Melissa Dalley, Gold Coast

ISBN 978-1-875468-00-3

TESTIMONIALS

Pastor Assemblies of God Church, Canberra, ACT: Thank you for your ministry, publications and newsletters. I believe in what you are doing and the essential need for a trans-denominational stance...in genuine love and concern I want your ministry to succeed.

Former Director of Evangelism, Queensland Baptist Union: Fred provides a valuable teaching ministry on cults and the New Age Movement. His ministry has been appreciated and helpful and is much needed within our churches. The teaching of cults today calls for pastors to teach our people the dangers. Our people need to be trained to handle the Word of Truth. The growing teaching of the cults and New Age emphasis today calls for us to teach our people the dangers of false teachings. I highly recommend Fred and the services he makes available.

Yvonne Snodgrass, VON Ministries, Florida, USA: I was blessed to hear the testimonies from both of you. The time is short and His Word says to work while it is day for night cometh when no man may work. I am with you in your ministry and would like to encourage you in whatever God has shown you to do. It was my privilege to have made contact with you at the League of Prayer Convention in Montgomery, Alabama, USA. God bless you.

Anglican Minister, Sydney: Thanks for your visit to our local Ministers' Fraternal. We all found your talk very revealing: it was extremely helpful to us all.

Former Pastor and AOG National Superintendent: I believe you have a great gift for the edification of the Body of Christ...I am willing to do all I can to speak to others and encourage them to have you minister.

Former Principal, Sydney Missionary and Bible College: Thank you for your assistance in the College program over these past three years. Your wide knowledge and personal experience of the cults made a valuable contribution to the student's preparation for Christian ministry.

Pastor, Semaphore, South Australia: We had a great time with you both and the folk were blessed with your ministry and the recent church split was restored. Once again, thank you for coming. Every blessing on your ministry.

Pastor and Former AOG NSW State Secretary: Pastor Grigg's ministry in exposing the problems with cults has greatly blessed our fellowship.

Pastor, Baptist Church, Baulkham Hills, Sydney: Fred is a man of considerable moral courage with a grasp of issues of conscience. He is a man of Integrity and profound Christian commitment. He has lectured and preached to Baptist audiences in various places in Sydney – always with great acceptance.

DISCLAIMER

The information published in this book is intended to be a general reference. I, Frederick R. Grigg, Chairman of Mandate Ministries Pty Ltd and author of this book, make the information and my comments available on the understanding that I am not thereby engaged in rendering professional advice.

I make every reasonable effort to maintain current and accurate information, hence this update and revision which becomes the 7th Edition. Readers should carefully evaluate the accuracy, currency, completeness and relevance of the information in this book for their own purposes, before relying on the material in any matter or circumstance. Readers should always obtain any appropriate professional advice relevant to their own particular circumstances.

I encourage readers to check with me if they have any concern about the information provided in this book. The links I have provided to websites are provided for my reader's' convenience. I do not accept responsibility for the information on any web site beyond the Mandate Ministries Website. In some cases the material may incorporate or summarise views, standards, or recommendations of third parties. Such material is assembled and presented in good faith, but does not necessarily reflect my views, or those who are associated with Mandate Ministries, nor does it indicate a commitment to a particular course of action.

Unless otherwise noted, all Scripture references are from The Holy Bible, New King James Version®, Copyright © 1994, Thomas Nelson Bibles, a Division of Thomas Nelson, Inc.

"It takes God a long time to get us to stop thinking that unless everyone sees things exactly as we do, they must be wrong. That is never God's view. There is only one true liberty - the liberty of Jesus at work in our conscience enabling us to do what is right. Don't get impatient with others. Remember how God dealt with you - with patience and with gentleness. But never water down the truth of God. Let it have its way and never apologize for it. Jesus said, "Go . . . and make disciples . . ." (Matthew 28:19), not, "Make converts to your own thoughts and opinions."

—Oswald Chambers - My Utmost for His Highest - May 6.

TABLE OF CONTENTS

Foreword		9
1.	Introduction and Explanation	11
2.	Staying on the Right Track	51
3.	Cults - Dead End of Deception	59
4.	Six Cult Danger Signals	71
5.	A Word about the Occult	79
6.	Is There Another Jesus?	89
7.	About Cult Leadership	103
8.	The Three Christological Heresies	111
9.	The Division of Heresies	119
10.	The Biblical Christ	133
11.	When Confronted by the Cultist	139
12.	How Then Should We Deal with Them?	143
13.	Extra-Biblical Revelation	155
14.	Some Probing Questions for the Cultist	167
15.	Confronting the Cultist	169
16.	Some Do's and Don'ts	179
17.	Scriptural Steps to Set People Free	189
18.	How to Become a True Christian	199
19.	Know Your Position in Christ	223
20.	Summary and Conclusion	231
21.	The Author's Short Story	237

Appendices:

1. Ten Signals That Say, "You Are Not Welcome in this Church" — 255

2.	The 'Jesus is Yahweh Wheel'	262
3.	The Seventh-day Adventist 'Clear Word Bible' + Jesus and Michael the Archangel	263
4.	The Greek Preposition *'en"* Chart	266
5.	The Greek Preposition *'en'* Illustration	267
6.	The Vietnam War 'TET Offensive'	268
7	Religions That Deny the Trinity	271

FOREWORD

I had been in pastoral ministry for some years when in 1981 I saw the need to write a book to support a new avenue of ministry which the Lord was beginning to open up to me. Never for one moment at that time did I ever think that here I would be, in late 2014, still revising and updating that original work, which I first published in 1982! Mandate Ministries became Australia's first 'counter-cult' ministry!

With my precious wife, Barbara, we have travelled extensively in ministry within Australia and overseas. It has been a privilege and a blessing to present the truth of God's Word to thousands of people and to be invited to preach and lecture in many different churches and numerous Bible colleges.

Many TV and radio programs, women's magazines, major city and regional newspapers have sought our advice over the years. They regard us as being qualified commentators on aberrant religious matters. We have had to confirm and verify the terrible experiences hurting people had shared with them about their involvement with false and dangerous religious groups. We have researched and authored many articles about the various beliefs, teachings and practices of many false religions, cults and the occult.

This revision is the Seventh. I wrote the book initially to warn and help Christians. However, with this update the book will hopefully accommodate the non-Christian reader and help them. The sources for this book come from personal experience and a lifetime of interest in studying and researching world religions.

Fred Grigg,
Gold Coast
September 2014

THE SCRIPTURAL CHALLENGE

"There are two paths before you; you may take only one path. One doorway is narrow. And one door is wide. Go through the narrow door. For the wide door leads to a wide path, and the wide path is broad; the wide, broad path is easy, and the wide, broad, easy path has many, many people on it; but the wide, broad, easy, crowded path leads to death. Now then that narrow door leads to a narrow road that in turn leads to life. It is hard to find that road. Not many people manage it.

"Along the way, watch out for false prophets. They will come to you in sheep's clothing, but underneath that quaint and innocent wool, they are hungry wolves. But you will recognize them by their fruits. You don't find sweet, delicious grapes growing on thorny bushes, do you? You don't find delectable figs growing in the midst of prickly thistles. People and their lives are like trees. Good trees bear beautiful, tasty fruit, but bad trees bear ugly, bitter fruit. A good tree cannot bear ugly, bitter fruit; nor can a bad tree bear fruit that is beautiful and tasty. And what happens to the rotten trees? They are cut down. They are used for firewood. When a prophet comes to you and preaches this or that, look for his fruits: sweet or sour? rotten or ripe?

"Not everyone who says to Me, "Lord, Lord," will enter the kingdom of heaven. Simply calling Me "Lord" will not be enough. Only those who do the will of My Father who is in heaven will join Me in heaven. At the end of time, on that day of judgment, many will say to Me, "Lord, Lord, did we not prophesy in Your name? Did we not drive demons out of the possessed in Your name? Did we not perform miracles in Your name?" But I will say to them, "I never knew you. And now, you must get away from Me, you evildoers!"

(Matthew 7:13 -27 The Voice, Thomas Nelson Inc.)

CHAPTER ONE

Introduction and Explanation

I believe it's very important to understand at the very beginning that mankind was created to be a naturally gregarious being and that normally he enjoys being in the company of others. I also believe that for a person to live in isolation, perhaps like a hermit, is not natural. Even God himself said, in Genesis 2:18, *'...the Lord God said, "It is not good that man should be alone..."'*.

There is nothing new about people gathering together in tribes, clans, congregations, teams, clubs, small groups and even gangs.[1] In my early years of schooling, we quite naturally formed ourselves into small groups. The members of those groups we would call our 'best friends', or 'mates'. So to live, work and play with a group of people who have good intentions and look out for each other is a very healthy and advantageous thing to have.

However, a cult group can have members from different religious and non-religious backgrounds and they all seem to get along well with each other and can be very supportive of one another. In this book I want to draw your attention to those who would call you out of your existing healthy relationships and into a relationship with a group which may want, even demand, you to abandon your family, friends, job, church or club and commit

---

[1] Throughout this book I will be using words like aberrant, group, cultic, cult group and dangerous groups, which can be equally interchanged and refer to a group that may be either religious or non-religious.

yourself exclusively to them. People who encourage you to take such a drastic course of action will lead you into problems that you never needed or envisaged you would have in the first place!

There are many groups, which form and align themselves around ideologies that were, or are being promoted by their founders and leaders. They come equally from religious and non-religious backgrounds and usually have compelling charm and charisma, which they use to inspire the devotion of others solely to themselves. In many instances, with the passage of time, such leaders developed extremes of conduct and activity for their groups to engage in. It is the methods which they use to achieve their ideals, their extremes and when they become known, are surprisingly very familiar and common in one form or another in most dangerous cultic groups down through the centuries.

It is because of such extremes and practices, which were being exhibited by a group at some point in time, which usually were first recognized by those who lived in the same geographical region where the group first had its beginnings. At some stage 'word had gotten out' into the local community that the members of the group were doing things that were invariably spiritually in error! Such things seemed quirky, weird, overly religious, super-spiritual, mind-controlling and sometimes they had become physically dangerous and therefore to be avoided. Members of some groups were easily recognized as they dressed differently. Unfortunately, for many people who involved themselves with some groups, it would eventually cost them their lives, both in this one and the one yet to come!

If one turns to the historical record, one will see that it clearly shows that there have always been extreme and dangerous groups active on this planet down through the ages. Their notoriety came about due to many similar factors. Perhaps the main factor which enables the birth of a cult is that there is no accountability of the leaders to a higher authority! Therefore, it would be true to say that any group that is not accountable to anyone has the potential to become aberrant, or markedly different and separated from the norm. Aberrancy usually comes about when a group, which may have had perfectly good legitimate reasons and very good intentions when they first began, changed their original belief system; changed their leadership; changed their lifestyle; or changed their geographical location! All these things are usually done to the detriment of the group's followers, or devotees.

The word 'aberrant' applies because any group that splits and strays from what is considered by society at the time as being acceptable and normal. Often they were classified as being aberrant by the very organization, or denomination, in which they had their roots. Such were often seen by local citizenry as being divisive and a people in rebellion. Eventually, such groups were exposed publicly for what they had become. Once public exposure took place, revealing their deviant teachings and practices, the group would soon be branded, or labelled by others, usually by word of mouth, as being a cult!

Initially, those who were delegated to expose such groups were usually drawn from respected and learned people in positions of authority in the community. If the group causing people concern was a 'religious' one, it was usually confronted by two or three concerned and appointed leaders from among the local churches. If they weren't a 'religious' group, then it would be likely that those who did the confronting would be drawn from senior and respected leaders and people of authority in the community.

Public exposure, in most instances, was always seen as being necessary in order to warn people not to get involved with a group. In most cases, public exposure occurred after there had been a determined effort made to meet with the erring group's leaders in order to discuss and express concerns, with a view to reconciliation. Sadly, what usually happens is that the group which was approached, invariably and stubbornly, rejects the wise counsel which was being offered to them! What resulted was that the group tended to become even further isolated and in due course eventually earned for themselves the label of being exclusive and therefore cultic in their beliefs and practices!

Historical records provide us with extensive and precise details as to the beginnings, or the roots, of many cultic and non-religious cult groups. Many of the older cult groups have managed to survive the passage of time and are still functioning quite openly, with others even covertly, in society today. If one makes the effort to research any group that claims exclusivity, they will be rewarded by being able to fully understand why they should have absolutely nothing to do with them!

For those of us who live in Western countries, we have efficient public libraries in most communities, which also provide free access to the Internet in blocks of time. So there's no excuse, or difficulty, for most of us to gain the insights we need into any of the cultic and dangerous religious and non-religious groups that we may be confronted by today. Sadly, most of the world's population live in disadvantaged countries, where those free libraries and Internet connections are not readily available, or if they are, they are unaffordable to the average person. This is why I believe that we, who live in the more affluent countries of the world, need to accept the responsibility of taking and making information like that contained in this book, available to them. Then they could learn for themselves how to avoid the deception of the cults and mind-controlling groups which can so easily deceive them through their lack of knowledge and their inability to gain it!

With the free and readily available resources that we have in society today, we can easily learn for ourselves how to negotiate the many spiritual and psychological 'minefields' which have been created by dangerous groups. Such groups are all vying for our attention and trying to convince us that we should become one of them! There is nothing about dangerous religions and cults that has changed down through the generations. We have noticed in our research that almost exactly the same deceptions seem to keep 'popping-up' again and again, in one form or another, as each new generation comes along![2]

There is much spiritual and physical evidence on the record which shows that <u>dangerous cultic groups always leave a trail of human wreckage behind them</u>! That 'human wreckage' consists of real people, just like you and me. They come from all walks of life, and have been harmed and damaged spiritually, emotionally, financially, physically, and very often sexually abused by a member or the leader/s of a cult group. Some have even lost their lives for what eventually proved to be displaced loyalty on their part. Former members of many groups would agree that they learnt the error of their ways far too late and they still bear the scars, inwardly, to prove it!

We should always be on the alert and watchful for cultic groups which lay claim - to any person who shows an interest in listening to what they have to say - that their group has the only way that one should follow in this life! They make statements like;

---

[2] The 'master deceiver, Satan the devil, obviously believes, "If at first I don't succeed, I will try and try again"!

"Ours is the only true way that leads a person into Everlasting Life" or, "It's only our way which will enable you to reach a higher level of enlightenment" and so on. There have been several groups, in the author's lifetime, who have dared to presumptuously claim, "We are the only people on earth with whom God is dealing with and speaking through today!"

Invariably, those who became involved with such groups and eventually left, when questioned as to why they joined the group in the first place, will invariably say, when asked, that they neglected to make a real effort to look into the group's roots! Many know nothing of their group's original teachings and its practices! Like many do, they simply accepted what they were being told because the people were so nice and friendly! Many now wish, including myself, that we had looked more closely into the claims that were being made to us by the group's members who we finished up being deceived by!

From both my wife's and my own experience, there are no doubts in our minds at all, that had we done some proper research for ourselves - and as said, we've had the same comment from those we have met, we would have discovered that almost all of the claims that were being made by the ones who approached and befriended us, were in fact, wrong! If we had done so back then, we would probably have realised, that what they were offering us amounted to nothing more than 'pie in the sky'! I'm absolutely positive that had we made the effort to fully check them out on the things that they were saying, which so appealed to us at the time, we would never have joined with them!

Perhaps the most common thing that we've found, is that what most cultic groups do for their followers, is to provide and make for their people, a means to escape the realities of life! We did not understand back then that the 'storms of life' affect everybody from time-to-time and that no one is exempt.

Research conducted by myself and many others, has established that most cults have, as stated before, had to change and alter many of their original teachings (doctrines) and practices (methodologies) with the passage of time. Why? Because, if they didn't make changes to what was their group originally believed, taught, and practiced, it would remain a continuing source of embarrassment to them and for the people whom they anticipated would join with and follow them in the future.

There is absolutely no argument at all on my part, that the majority of the followers of cultic groups are very fine, very sincere, very committed, and very loyal people! However, what they have done, except for those born and raised in a cult, is to unwittingly allow themselves to be swept into what I call a 'spiritual backwater' – as the reader already knows, backwaters go nowhere and become stagnant!

I believe there have been two major curses with which mankind has been blighted. The first, is that since the first man and woman, Adam and Eve, rebelled against God and disobeyed him and fell from grace in the Garden of Eden,[3] that false religion has spread its tentacles to all points of the compass! The second, has been the desire for people to have power and control over other people for their own advantage, physically, morally, and more often than not, financially.

The teachings and practices of those who try to convince others that they are the only ones who are on the 'right path' or have the 'best and only way' eventually leads the group's members to one conclusion and that is that they are right and everyone else

---

[3] Genesis 3:1-24

therefore must be wrong! This attitude is one that further 'isolates' one to the group. It is often the cause of great confusion for some who have to leave their family and friends behind. True Christians know who 'the author of confusion' is – they will tell you that it comes from none other than the one who is referred to in the Bible, as being 'the father of lies'! Which of course is none other the devil, or Satan himself![4] The Bible states that Satan is the 'Prince who rules this world! (The Greek word for 'world' is '*kosmos*' and I'll have more to say about the *kosmos* later!)

Satan has a large following of lesser spirits who are his cohorts in evil, which are named correctly as 'demonic spirits.' They are also deceivers and liars. No, by my saying that I haven't just gone 'loopy' on you, in fact I am deadly serious! Please note what the Apostle Paul said in one of his letters in the Bible (which is the inspired Word of God), about what Christians should do to counter the work of Satan and his evil spirit beings who want nothing other than to steal and kill and destroy[5] the good things that a loving God wants mankind to have in their lives:

"Finally, my brethren, be strong in the Lord and in the power of His might. Put on the whole armour of God that you may be able to stand against the wiles of the devil. For we do not wrestle against flesh and blood, but against principalities, against powers, against the rulers of the darkness of this age, against spiritual hosts of wickedness in the heavenly places." (Ephesians 6:10-12)

---

[4] Ephesians 2:1-2 The writer is speaking to Christians, *"And you He made alive, who were dead in trespasses and sins, in which you once walked according to the course of this world (kosmos), according to <u>the prince of the power of the air</u>, the spirit who now works in the sons of disobedience..."*

[5] John 10:10

The reality is, that people who join cultic groups have absolutely no idea what they have unwittingly opened themselves up to? Without them realising it they have placed themselves under the influence of what is termed, 'a spirit of deception'. If one reads the first four books of the New Testament in the Bible – written by the Apostles of Jesus, Matthew, Mark, Luke and John, you will see that Jesus Christ believed very much in the existence of evil spirits! Why? Because the authors record for us the fact that he frequently set people free from bondage to them. He did this simply by taking authority over them and casting them out, telling them never to return![6]

This is why it can be very difficult for people who come to a point where they can 'see' for themselves that they need to leave the cult they belong to, but for some reason just can't bring themselves to make the decision to actually do it! Why? It's simply because of the demonic influence which holds them in spiritual bondage. Such bondage is very strong and very difficult to break away from in your own strength. However, many have shared with us, when they were going through that experience, they became aware, or had a 'nagging feeling' when they were first getting involved with the group which made them feel very uneasy. That uneasiness was what some would call their, 'gut instinct'. I would believe that it could also have been the Holy Spirit telling them that there was 'something wrong with the group', but they had no way of realizing it at the time?

My wife and I both had that 'nagging feeling' and it was one that seemed to come back to us from time-to-time. It

---

[6] Luke 8:26-32 The account of the Gadarene demon-possessed man being set free from the demonic and healed! (Also recorded in Mark 5:1-20)

surfaced frequently when something happened in the JW group we were in, or some teaching that we didn't quite agree with or understand was given. For some, as it did for me, it motivated me to begin asking questions of those I felt I could trust in the group.

Some have told me that they started doing some secretive research for themselves. They usually did this when they were alone and not being 'watched'! Slowly, as the Holy Spirit began His 'ministry' in them and in us and God the Father began to draw us to Himself, we would come to understand, little by little, that the group which once filled us with great hopes and expectations for the future, could never deliver on what they had promised!

Coming to that conclusion and being in such an emotional state of mind, as is often the case, when the person seeks help from those they thought were close friends in the group, they were usually betrayed and 'dobbed in'[7] to the elders or leader! The leaders of course, would then speak with them 'officially' and they may even discipline them by placing restrictions on them in ways that would usually humiliate them in front of other members. For some, when the disciplinary process began, it would be rejected and they would pluck up the courage to leave.

When they left the group, the leaders would always discourage others from relating to them at all! When this happens to someone, others in the group, perhaps for the first time, would become aware of what would happen to them if they should ever think about leaving. This only makes it harder for them when things become difficult when they begin to have similar 'niggling thoughts' about leaving the group.

---

[7] A 'dobber' is someone who secretly tells someone in authority what someone else has done or said.

Many who seek help will secretly choose someone with whom they may have an affinity with and believe they can trust outside the group. It could be a friend from the past or someone in their family who has not been critical or condemning of them. Sometimes it may even be a Christian who they may have come to know? Or, they may search with apprehension for a Christian to speak to because they feel the one they know is not equipped to help with a situation like they are in. Often, the one they turn to does have the faith and knowledge to set people free from the spiritual oppression and bondage in which they are entangled. You can only win spiritual battles by using spiritual weapons!

At some point in the on-going dilemma which a person may have, there comes a time when they seriously begin to think, "Should I stay, or should I go? Such a question naturally creates in them fears and worries. Fear of being found out; fear of being alone if they leave[8]; worry about the consequences, both pro and con! From our own experience, and those who have shared with us, it seems to be 'par for the course' that when a person decides to leave a cult and tries to do so, that they find it extremely difficult to actually make the decisive decision to break away.

Why is this? It's simply because when a person joins with a cultic group it is not a matter of his intelligence, or lack of it, as many would have you believe that compelled him to join! Some of the most intelligent minds on earth have been unknowingly deceived and many of them became, or are currently leaders of cult groups that have huge followings! As said before, there is a 'spiritual chain of bondage' which needs to be broken from them in order to set them free! Even though a person may physically

---

[8] There is a big difference being 'alone' and being 'lonely'.

leave a group, there is always a spiritual bond that needs to be broken in order for them to be totally set free. Let me illustrate it this way:

Years ago, at a seminar I was conducting in Toowoomba, a man came up to me at the end of a session where I exposed the errors of the Jehovah's Witnesses. He said, "Thanks for coming, you're the first one who has explained to me that the decision I made 12 years ago to leave the Witnesses was totally right."!

In another instance, I said to a young man, who had finally come to the understanding that the 'church' he was fellowshipping with was wayward and controlling, "Robert,"[9] I asked, "Now that you know that the church is in error and there is nobody holding a gun to your head to make you stay. Why don't you just simply walk away and never go back?" Looking downcast at the floor, he despondently replied, "I've really thought I should leave several times, but I just can't seem to actually do it. I'm afraid that if I do, that something bad is going to happen to me! It's like as if I'm being held in a prison without bars"!

For me, what he said was clear evidence that Robert was being controlled by what I named earlier, a 'deceiving spirit'. In his case I believe it was coupled with a companion spirit, a 'spirit of fear'! Both of which were responsible for keeping him in spiritual bondage. He shared with me that he had spoken to someone in the church privately about his feelings. They apparently ostracized him and told him that if he left, he would not receive the healing that he had been trusting and hoping for! I knew he would only be able to 'walk away' and be free when the power of the two spirits, and any others that may be oppressing him, was broken and they

---

[9] Not his real name

were voluntarily on his part, were cast out of his life forever!

Because of circumstances that were beyond his control, Robert had become a very 'perplexed and confused' man. He was skeptical about almost everything. I went on to explain to him and tried to assure him that if he didn't feel up to praying with me that day, that he could come back another time? I told him that he could even pray for himself, as some we know have done, when he felt up to it. I said that by simply praying a prayer out loud in which he should re-affirm his commitment to Jesus being his Saviour and Lord. Then he should denounce and renounce the 'spirit of deception' and the 'spirit of fear' that were in his life and command them to leave and never return (I also explained to him there may be others that were perhaps affecting him?). I suggested he also renounce the spirits of control the leaders of the church were exercising over him and others. Knowing that this was a lot to ask, I then said to him that perhaps, if he could not bring himself to do so and if he felt comfortable, he could ask a mature Christian friend that he may have - but not from his 'church' - to assist him by praying with him when he was ready, or he could come back to us?

Become an Investigator: When one digs down into the 'roots' of any group that one may suspect of being cultic, it will invariably reveal one of two things. Firstly, it will establish the roots and erroneous teachings and practices of the group. Or, secondly, it may prove, that the group in question, was not dangerous at all and that it had just been misunderstood by some, which can be a good thing. If one finds that to be the case, then one may have to take a long and hard look at themselves to find the reasons which may have put them out of step with what was perhaps a good church in the first place?

As inferred, such research sometimes reveals what the

group believed and taught in the days when they first began. When I came to this point in my situation of researching the JW's, I discovered that there were some very ludicrous and very revealing things that had been published in their early books and magazines, particularly about the their initial beliefs and teachings![10] If it wasn't so serious, what they had written and published would be laughable! Remember, the enemy of error is always the passage of time. Time will always prove to cult members that their hopes were based on nothing but false and erroneous teachings. As alluded to, many people eventually come to an understanding that their hopes were false and only existed in the minds of their founder/s, or the group's subsequent leaders!

When this realisation occurs, as it often does for many cult group followers, any credibility that they may have had in their leader's integrity is immediately dashed! There comes with this an awful sense that they have been conned, duped, and ripped-off! Then the realization that all of their energies, time and money, which they had expended so freely and given so willingly to the 'cause' of the group, perhaps faithfully over a period of many years, had all been for nothing! For most people who have spent time in a cult, all they have to show for their years of commitment, faithful service, and their giving financially to their

---

[10] For many years the JW's claimed they had 'another witness' that was written in stone? That 'Witness' proved to be the Great Pyramid of Giza in Egypt! From measuring the lengths of certain passages inside the pyramid – from one chamber to another - and then calling every inch a year, they came up with the first of their many failed dates - 1874! In Studies in the Scriptures – The Divine Plan of the Ages, 1924, p6, *"...we are living in the time of the second presence of our Lord, and that presence dates from 1874; that since that time we have been living in the "time of the end," the "end of the age" during which the Lord has been conducting his great harvest work..."*

group amounted to nothing but a so-called 'hill of beans'!

Sadly, what actually begins for the person at this time is what I now call, 'The Mind Games'. I know how difficult and draining emotionally and mentally such 'games' can be! One experiences a range of mixed thoughts which constantly invade, or flood into one's mind. You have feelings of loneliness and even a fear of being alone; you experience great sadness and loss; you feel bitterness and even anger; you feel hollow and empty; you experience disconnectedness; you feel frustrated, you feel foolish and even shame! Why shame? Because you think you are just plain stupid for allowing yourself to so gullibly 'be led up the garden path'!

This can often lead them and their loved ones into experiencing further tragedy and loss. This is where for many the 'spiritual side' we've spoken of really begins to 'kick in'! Evil spirits will not give up without putting up a fight! Jesus himself told us that bad news comes from the 'evil one', known as the 'thief', *"The thief does not come except to steal, and to kill, and to destroy."* However, the good news comes thankfully in the second half of the same verse, where Jesus continues and says, *"I have come that they may have life, and that they may have it more abundantly."*[11]

That is truly a great promise! A promise which is made to all who make the decision to turn to him, whether they are trapped in a cult or not. Jesus said that He only is the Way, the Truth and the Life[12] In fact, I believe beyond any shadow of doubt that the answer to the cult explosion can only found in the true Lord Jesus Christ, the Son of the Living God!

---

[11] John 10:10
[12] John 14:6

With all of the foregoing things and more going on in a person's mind, is it any wonder that he or she eventually succumbs to and is afflicted by depression! I was depressed for a very long time and many others have told me they were too when they went through this same state on indecision! The dilemma we faced was compounded when the 'spirits of deception' in our lives had what I would now call 'a field day' in the battleground of our mind! Sadly, there are many, who have never been effectively counselled spiritually are not truly free. Because of this they are spiritually stalled at this stage of life and many and are under psychiatric care for what has been labelled as being "their emotional and behavioral problems". Many have probably been dosed up, by those who prescribe, with anti-depressant drugs – which in my experience do absolutely nothing to address their real spiritual problems and needs! The majority of the medical profession do not know that it's impossible to medicate a person who is being troubled by 'evil spirits'!

A major tactic that the 'spirit realm' uses is to unrelentingly trouble and scramble the thoughts of a person, both day and night. They bring back distressing memories and dreams which will pour into their mind questions like: should I leave the group; am I at fault; should I hang in and hope for the best; if I leave, I will probably have to leave all my friends and/or family behind (because they may not see things in the same way the questioning person does); where will I go; how will I survive; If I leave I will lose the job they gave me when I joined; I'll probably be killed in an accident as I will no longer have God's protection; how will I find another job at my age; how will I cope with being alone; how could I face my family and former friends after all that I've said to them in the past when I tried to get them to join with my group and be with me?

Perhaps the most troubling thoughts, as mentioned, are where some of the member's immediate family, who may have been influenced by the person to join the group with them when they did, is the question, "If I leave now, I know they will be counselled by the leaders to remain true and loyal to the group. I know they will encourage them to cut me off and have nothing more to do with me!"

For emphasis, I'll repeat it again; it is a fact that those who choose to ignore the warning signs, or those 'niggling thoughts' and the evidence gained at this stage and decide to hang in and hope for the best – as many do just to keep the peace - will invariably face a much more difficult time leaving further down the track. It's always a bad decision to stay in a group when you know that the group is wrong and in error! Why? To answer that question and by way of illustration, consider the following four scenarios:

The Jehovah's Witnesses (JW's)

Firstly, have you ever wondered, what has become of the many thousands of disillusioned people who left the JW's after years of being encouraged and coerced by their leaders, under the direction of their 'Governing Body' based at that time in Brooklyn, New York, to eagerly look forward to what has now become just another one of their multitude of failed dates – the last major one being October 14-15th 1975![13] JW's around the world were

---

[13] At the 1967 JW District Convention, in Wisconsin USA, Sheboygan District Overseer Charles Sunutko, spoke on the subject of, "Serving with Everlasting Life in View", during which he made the following statement: *"Well now, as Jehovah's Witnesses, as runners, even though some of us have become a little*

looking forward to that date with great anticipation and hope! *"Today there is a great crowd of people who are confident that a destruction of even greater magnitude is now imminent. The evidence is that Jesus' prophecy will shortly have a major fulfilment, upon this entire system of things. This has been a major factor in influencing many couples to decide not to have children at this time."* Awake! 1974 Nov 8 p.11

Note the following JW Timeline Chart published by the Watchtower Society:

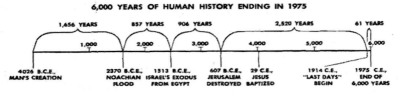

JW Awake Magazine 15 Aug 1968 inferring 'the End' would occur in 1975

The Jehovah's Witnesses were repeatedly confronted with what 1975 would mean for them, it would be, "…(T)he beginning of the Battle of Armageddon with the glorious outcome being the end of this evil system of things in which we live and the setting up Jehovah's Kingdom on earth"! It is interesting to note that the Watchtower Society itself says that the standard by which to judge a false messenger is whether or not their messages "come true"? The following is a quote is from The Watchtower Magazine, May

---

weary, it almost seems as though Jehovah has provided meat in due season. Because he's held up before all of us, a new goal. A new year. Something to reach out for and it just seems it has given all of us so much more energy and power in this final burst of speed to the finish line. <u>*And that's the year 1975.*</u> *Well, we don't have to guess what the year 1975 means if we read the Watchtower. And don't wait 'till 1975. The door is going to be shut before then. As one brother put it, "Stay alive to Seventy-Five..."* (From an audio recording in the author's possession.)

1, 1997 p.8: "Jehovah is the Grand identifier of his true messengers. He identifies them by making the messages he delivers through them come true. Jehovah is also the Great Exposer of false messengers."

They were led to believe that it would be only the JW's who would survive the coming Battle of Armageddon in 1975! Immediately after that Battle, they were taught, they would all be tasked with the setting up of 'a new system of things' with them having the task of restoring the Earth to its former glorious 'paradise condition' – i.e., just as it was back in the Garden of Eden before Adam and Eve's disobedience, which was to cause their subsequent fall!

I know that before the anticipated date in October 1975, many sincere and faithful JW's gave up what were very well-paying jobs which they had held for many years! Many sold their businesses and houses; many young adults dropped out of university and others left high school as soon as they were legally old enough; most gave freely of their money and time 'as a sign of their faith' to do what was expected of them by the Watchtower Society, which of course was to "Publish the Good News about the end of this System of Things in 1975"!

They were expected to sell and/or give away Watchtower books and magazines – which of course they had to buy from their Kingdom Halls first – as they went from house-to-house and door-to-door! Many were challenged to move to other congregations that were smaller in numbers, or move to regional cities and towns. This was done under a strategic plan which was named, 'Serving Where the Need is Greater'. Many JW's would boast, as if it were some sort of status symbol that they were planning, "We're going to serve where the need is greater"! Some believed it was an outward sign to others of their commitment and obedience to 'Jehovah's Organisation' and they had to go! They were encouraged by their leaders, here in Australia, to even move to places of high unemployment – naturally, places where vulnerable people live! The leaders knew the JW's would not readily be able to find employment and they encouraged them that they would be well able to survive on unemployment benefits - the then Social Security Dole payment! They were told, "The Government will pay you to spend your work time going from house to house in your Field Service"!

All this was supervised and controlled so that as many members as possible would be more active in promoting and selling their books and magazines! Every Kingdom Hall congregation member, including young children and the very elderly were expected, if it was at all physically possible, to trudge from house-to-house speaking to anyone who would listen to them, for a minimum of 8 hours, on average, per month. They were encourage to do even more if they could do so! Would you believe that Queensland's Gold Coast became the most popular place to 'serve where the need was greater'? It was so popular, that the JW national leaders, in their monthly 'Our Kingdom Ministry' newsletter, instructed members to stop going to the Gold Coast as there was, "No longer a need there"!

There were other volunteers in Field Service who were called 'Pioneers'. They had to commit themselves to an average of 120+ hours per month! Pioneers were held in high regard by the JW's. Being a Pioneer tended to give them a revered status in the eyes of the rank-and-file. However, if they didn't achieve their target, unless there was a good reason why they didn't, they would also be counselled by the leaders shape up! However, with all the emphasis being given to the Year 1975 all it eventually proved to be for them another great disappointment! One more failed date for the JW's to add to their infamous score of failed prophecies![14]

The Rajneesh Movement - aka 'The Orange People'

Secondly, what now of the former extremely zealous and very colourful people who were once known as the 'Orange People'? They sincerely gave their all to follow the now long deceased Indian Hindu Guru who was and is still known in India as 'Osho' (b: Chandra Mohan Jain, 11 Dec1931, d.1990) who became better known to the world as Bhagwan Shree Rajneesh.

In the 1970's and early 1980's his devotees numbered in the thousands. With his follower's money, he established a large commune (Hindu: Ashram) in the town of The Dalles in Oregon, USA. The movement imploded in a cloud of corruption and murder allegations.[15] Almost overnight the Orange People seemed to disappear. It was disbanded shortly after November 1985, when the then 54 year-old Baghwan was deported from the USA and had to return to India due to immigration charges. Amongst many other indulgences, at one stage, he reportedly had a fleet of about ninety (90) Rolls Royce luxury cars! It was reported that his followers were planning to give him a total of 365 – one for his personal use for every day of the year!

---

[14] Significant, incorrect and false Watchtower Dates quoted from various Watchtower publications: B.C. 607, 539 A.D. 1780, 1798, 1799, 1829, 1840, 1844, 1846, 1872, 1874, 1878, 1880, 1881, 1891, 1906, 1910, 1914, 1915, 1917, 1918, 1920, 1921, 1925, 1926, 1928, 1932, 1935, 1940's, 1957, 1975, 2000 (Sadly, one could say, "Watch this space for the next JW date!)

[15] http://www.abc.net.au/compass/s3795813.htm 29 Apr 2014

A number of his Western devotees moved with him when he returned to India. However, the majority of them chose to remain in the US and tried to unsuccessfully continue on. Eventually, there was only a small remnant. In a very short time, they gave up wearing their orange clothing and re-named themselves as being the, 'Rainbow People'! They began wearing clothes of many colours! Time of course, as said before, always proves to be the enemy of all cultic groups. Eventually, lacking the charismatic leadership like Bhagwan's, the devotees simply gave up and went back into their former ways, or melded into other like-minded Eastern religious groups.

The People's Temple

Thirdly, what of the survivors and the many disillusioned people of the now infamous American church, 'The Peoples Temple of the Disciples of Christ'? Authors Phil Kearns and Doug Wead co-authored a book about the church having the title, "People's Temple – People's Tomb'![16] This group was led by a charismatic personality, the 'Reverend Jim Jones'. He was idolised by his followers. Many people in his meetings gave testimonies to their being kept from harm or being provided for by saying things like, "I give thanks to Jim Jones who saved me from being injured in a car wreck on the highway"! Jones was definitely a 'false christ'[17]

It was on the 18th November of 1978 that just over 900 of his people were to lose their lives after being encouraged by Jones to join him and move to establish a socialistic community which he

---

[16] Now unavailable and out of print – I will quote some principles from this book later.

[17] Mathew 7:21-23; 24:3-5 & 24-26

was developing in the jungles of Guyana in South America! Many of his US followers moved to Guyana to help and work for what Jones named the, 'Peoples Temple Agricultural Project'. Many said Jones claimed it would become a 'modern-day Utopia' and living there would be like Heaven on Earth!

When almost unbelievable accounts began to circulate about Jones's increasing control and worsening conduct towards his people in Guyana, it was then that his former good character and reputation in the USA began to tarnish. Accounts began to be told, when people returned to the States, about him and his leader's heinous acts of abuse. Some reports claimed that people were being beaten as punishment for minor 'misdemeanors'. Marriages and families were being separated and broken up.

In spite of the many 'rumours' circulating, his followers in the USA were still being encouraged to leave the States (and their non-church family members behind) and sell up and move to live in Guyana. Many who made the move left behind secure and well-paying jobs. Reports of many other evil deeds surfaced, which unfortunately were consistent and typical of what mind-controlling and unaccountable cult leaders can cause their group to devolve into!

Eventually, the authorities began to act and started to move on Jones in order to bring him to account. When they got too close for his comfort, Jones ordered all his followers who were then living with him in Guyana, to commit mass suicide! This command resulted in the death of hundreds! Jones's body was among the dead! It was an absolute massacre, with bodies strewn all over the grounds! Jones's followers, including the women and children, were forced to drink what was later proven to be a 'poisonous and deadly cocktail'! It was a <u>mixture of cyanide and valium</u>! These two ingredients were mixed with a grape juice named Flavor-Aid®, which is similar to the well-known drink, Kool-Aid®.

When the slaughter began, many refused to drink the concoction and were immediately shot dead by Jones's gunmen; others attempted to flee by trying to run and escape into the jungle. A small number did manage to escape and live to tell their story. Most were chased down, shot and killed! Some called it 'a mass suicide' but most rightly refer to it as being a 'mass murder'!

Heaven's Gate

Fourthly, on March 26th 1997 thirty-nine dead bodies were discovered, which included the group's leader and 38 others associated with a small group named, 'Heaven's Gate'. They were an American UFO religious millenarian group[18] based in San Diego, California, USA. The cult had its beginnings in the early 1970s and was led by one Marshall Herff Applewhite and woman named Bonnie Nettles.

Members of the small group, on the day appointed, donned their Nike© sport shoes and track suits and were led to commit yet another 'cult group suicide'! They were told and led to believe that when they 'passed over' (or 'died') they would be immediately be, "...transferred to link up with, and board an alien spacecraft..."! They were told by Applewhite the spacecraft was following in the 'wash', or tail, of the then passing Hale-Bopp Comet which was then at its brightest and closest to earth! The

---

[18] Millenarian groups typically claim that the current society and its rulers are corrupt, unjust, or otherwise wrong. They were taught and believed they would soon be destroyed by a powerful force. The harmful nature of the status quo is always considered intractable without the anticipated dramatic change.

Members believed that the earth was to be cleansed and recycled and that the only way for one to survive was to leave it immediately!

* * * *

By now you may by wondering how is it possible for a person to avoid such cunning and outlandish deceptions? The answer, and I repeat it yet again for emphasis, is that one should make the time to avail oneself of the ready access available in our libraries. They have reference works to consult about religious groups that are simply gathering dust on their shelves! Perhaps, if they don't have what you need about a certain group, you can ask for research help and probably, if they don't have it, they can get a loan copy of what you are looking for from another linked library. This means that a person, living in today's society really has no excuse for not being able to verify the teachings and practices of any religious group which could possibly have the potential to turn out to be just like those groups cited in the foregoing illustrations. However, many of the groups that most would classify as being dangerous, have unwittingly and to our advantage, created their own websites which one can easily go to and research for themselves[19]. There are also many well-meaning individuals, para-church ministries and many of the established and Biblically sound churches who have set up websites, not only to promote their own ministries, but also to provide information to assist and help others to avoid deception. They willingly promote truth and expose error to help others to be able to recognise cult groups and/or false teachings and practices. If you find that a group you

---

[19] I keep watch on many cults by simply subscribing to their email newsletters!

have researched does not credibility, even in one area of belief or practice, then you should avoid them at all cost.

Those who provide such information see themselves as simply providing helpful insights and information as a public service. Most do so at their own expense and for the common good just as we do. Many of those who expose and name dangerous cult groups, were once members of those very cults themselves. This of course means that they have first-hand knowledge and experience which is invaluable to assist and teach others how to avoid being deceived. They know what it's like to be held in spiritual bondage! Thankfully, we were set free and many of us were aided by people promoting the same principles which I have outlined in this book!

* * * *

Recently, I visited the Australian Bureau of Statistics (ABS) website concerning our 2011 National Census. Under Religious Affiliations I found that for the almost 23+ million people who now live in Australia, it stated that 61.1% of the population said they were Christian; 7.3% claimed to be from 'Other Religions'; 22.3% said they were of 'No Religion' and 9.3% chose not to respond to the question. What those percentages mean to us is that there has to logically be a very large number of active and dangerous religious groups functioning in society today. The majority of them proclaiming, promoting and peddling their own 'unique message' saying, "Come and join with us. If you don't you will be lost for all eternity" or similar!

Consider the dilemma the average person has today? Living in times of extreme adversity, with all the stress and anxieties that we are being bombarded with created by the media, where does one turn for answers and help? Many people are stressed-out and looking earnestly for answers to their own needs and others worried about the world's problems. How confusing must it be, over a period of time, when one has been confronted by people from many different groups and religions with every one of them proclaiming to be the only true representatives of God on Earth; or the only path to true enlightenment that one should be travelling on! Is it any wonder that when the true Christian Gospel is offered to them, that in their state of confusion, they sadly reject it outright and throw it out just like 'the baby with the bathwater'!

Following are just of some of the new types of questions which are being asked by people searching for the answers and/or the meaning to life? Of course, the 'standard questions' still get asked like, "Which church is the true church?" or, "Why are there so many different religions?" and, "If god is a god of love, then why is there so much killing and bloodshed going on in the world?" So, let's take a look at what I believe is a major root cause of today's dangerous religions and cults!

Multiculturalism – The Beginning of 'Political Correctness'

I believe that many of the questions people are wanting answers to in our society today, have come about due in part to the emphasis and pressure that was placed by the United Nations (UN) just a few years after the end of World War II, on its member nations, or states, to embrace and incorporate the concept which was given the name, 'Multiculturalism'. Today, various UN Agencies are still pushing and promoting for member states to adopt the concept!

The word 'multiculturalism' came out of the enormous problem created with the re-settling of the massive numbers of displaced persons and refugees created by the effects of the 1939-1945 World War II. This was due to the devastation created by six long years of world war, where multitudes of people were left homeless. Many were not able to return to their homes or homelands. Economic reasons were at the forefront. Adding to their problems was the fact that these people came from different cultural, language and religious backgrounds and therefore would, or could not, readily mix with others. Assisted emigration was the concept that was implemented to assist people financially to migrate and settle in other less war affected countries. Many chose to migrate because they were told they would be able to find and pursue a better lifestyle for themselves and their families. Even today, with millions of new refugees and displaced persons, various NGO relief agencies and the UN believe that such people should be helped to migrate and integrate into a country's populace. They do this in the hope that in two or three generations the immigrants would be assimilated into their new societies. For the many emigrants who settled in Australia from Europe after WWII, the vast majority of them assimilated well.

However, there were minorities, who out of necessity, established small enclaves in older city suburbs. In recent decades, with migrants coming from non-European countries, assimilation has proven not to be the case. Many who readily migrated soon learned after their arrival, that the ideals they were led to expect and hope for did not quickly materialise. Migrants in the late 1940's and early 1950's initially found themselves living in military barracks which became known as 'Migrant Hostels'. The associated difficulties of having many families living in accommodations that were designed originally for single military personnel were enormous. Although the 'boat people' (mostly queue jumpers) have now been stopped, of those who arrived under Labor Government policy, many now find themselves being deported or living in Detention Centres for long periods of time, or being sent back to where they came from!

Those who came legally, immediately after WWII, and now more recently, who do not have a reasonable command of English, find there is a 'language barrier' for them to overcome! In the early years in most States of Australia, the 'Migrant Hostels'[20] were located in the outer suburban areas of major cities. This meant that employment was difficult to find. Many faced discrimination and prejudice – particularly if they were from a former 'enemy' country! Many, both then and now, are unskilled. That with the aforementioned difficulties, with the language problem are almost unemployable. Many have no other option but to keep to themselves and look out for each other. Naturally, this means they are better able to maintain their own distinctive cultural and religious differences.

Many countries ignored the warnings of the complications as they urgently needed to boost their workforce numbers due to the decimating of their manpower from the effects of war! When problems began to arise many countries quickly introduced and passed urgent legislation that was designed to 'enshrine' non-discriminatory laws that the authorities hoped would enforce and create what some referred to as, "Societies that would be enabled to find 'Unity in their Diversity'". Emanating from Canada's immigration problems came the word 'Multicultural'! It was thought by many that legislation would guarantee the rights of migrants and help them to find equality in their new societies. It was interesting for the writer to note that the theme for the

---

[20] Many were established using the barracks of former military bases.

World Expo 88 Exhibition conducted in Brisbane in 1988 was 'Unity in Diversity'!

Multiculturalism was 'officially' introduced into Australia under the newly elected democratic socialist Prime Minister, Gough Whitlam (recently deceased) and his Labor Government of 1973. He implemented 'Multiculturalism' without any public support, or even consultation! Labor Member of Parliament, Al Grassby (1926- 2005), was appointed by the Prime Minister to be his new Minister for Immigration. His task was to implement the so-called 'reforms in immigration and human rights' that were perceived as being needed. For his efforts, Al Grassby is remembered today as, 'the father of Australian Multiculturalism'.

The Australian Department of Immigration has morphed through several name changes over the years. From 1996-2001 it was, the Department of Immigration and Multicultural Affairs. In 2001-2006 its name was changed to the Department of Immigration and Multicultural and Indigenous Affairs. In 2007-2013 it bore the name Department of Immigration and Citizenship! In 2013 it was changed yet again to its current name, the Department of Immigration and Border Protection – notice the word 'multicultural' has been dropped!
In Australia, as it is with other countries, from their bad experiences in trying to implement Multiculturalism, many in authority are now saying that Multiculturalism has proven to be nothing but a failure! In spite of this fact, UN agencies are still saying to anyone who will listen to them that, "Multiculturalism is a fact of life..."![21] It very interesting to note what well-known

---

[21] http://www.un-ngls.org/spip.php?page=article_s&id_article=3995 29 Apr 2014

Australian historian, Geoffrey Blainey,[22] now deceased, almost prophetically, wrote of multiculturalism in 1984, he said, "...(W)e should think very carefully about the perils of converting Australia into a giant multicultural laboratory for the assumed benefit of the peoples of the world." In one of his numerous criticisms of multiculturalism, Blainey wrote: "For the millions of Australians who have no other nation to fall back upon, multiculturalism is almost an insult. It is divisive. It threatens social cohesion. It could, in the long term, also endanger Australia's military security because it sets up enclaves which in a crisis could appeal to their own homelands for help."

Blainey's fears for Australia's future military security, since the end of the 2014 Sochi Winter Olympics in Russia, have been vividly portrayed with what has been happening in Ukraine with Crimea being annexed by Russia! Ukraine has been at war in the eastern part of the country with the mainly Russian speaking Ukranians (93%) who want to become part of the new Russian Federation! At the time of writing there is a very fragile and shaky ceasefire in place, with some serious violations on both sides being reported in the media. I won't go into the details here as the reader would know that as I write, there are now thousands of Russian troops in both Crimea and along the eastern border of Ukraine who are still intimidating and trying to force a split – the article posted on the website below[23] describes the build-up of what has

---

[22] Blainey, Geoffrey. "All For Australia", Methuen Haynes, North Ryde, N.S.W., 1984

[23] 'A Quick Guide to What's Happening in Ukraine':
http://online.wsj.com/news/articles/SB10001424052702303775504579393324230970300

been the obvious intent of the Russians for some time – and that is to add Ukraine to its new Federation!

Another example of the fulfilment of Patrick White's fears has surfaced in recent times regarding the many conflicts in the unstable Middle East. Under the headline "Disillusioned young Muslim men head to fight in Middle East,"[24] News.com says, "As many as 300 young Australians have left for the Middle East with hopes of joining the battles which have become some of the most savage the region has ever seen. The estimate — around three times greater than earlier calculations — has been made by sources close to families and communities in western Sydney. It was made before the Islamic States of Iraq and Syria ('ISIS', then 'Islamic States of Iraq and the Levant' and now just IS, for 'Islamic State') offensive, which threatens to see Baghdad become the site of a bloody sectarian showdown between the Shi'ite government and the Sunni insurgents. There are deep concerns the young men will be killed in fighting, or will survive and return with their religious zealotry heightened and having learned deadly military fighting skills that they might put to use at home..."

Just this week in Melbourne, a Muslim terrorist was shot dead as he tried to kill and behead two policemen, who were both hospitalized, due to their severe knife wounds! It was an act that was requested by leaders of IS in the Middle East!

What this means is that Australia's dalliance with 'multiculturalism' has failed terribly and has left our country with a legacy of people from many nations, with different cultures, foreign religions and agendas, with most not even interested in integrating into our society at all! For many, even though taking

---

[24] Published 17 Jun 2014 by News.com.au

out Australian citizenship, there is no doubt that their allegiance is still with the countries they originated from? Their country of origin citizenship takes priority over their citizenship here! Many of the so-called 'Home grown Australian Terrorists' who hold dual-citizenship have not done as they were expected to by our powers that be!

Since Great Britain established the first European settlement in Australia in 1788 we have had over 6.5 million settlers from 190+ nations who now live here permanently! Four out of ten Australians are migrants, or the first-generation children of migrants, half of whom have come from non-English speaking backgrounds. The only thing multiculturalism has achieved here is to create isolated communities, or enclaves, both in our cities and in many of our regional centres. As their numbers grew, in only a few short years, they have become the dominant residents of a suburb and are now encroaching on the surrounding suburbs. This is creating regions where they can now live out their own culture, practice their own religion, and speak their own language. Assimilation is simply a non-event! Many of these communities have become unofficial 'No Go Zones' for the average Aussie! In some reported instances even our law enforcement agencies are not welcome to enter!

To illustrate further what this legacy of multiculturalism has left us with. The following is from an article dated 21 July 2014 and headed, "Australia: Demonstrators denounce Israeli invasion of Gaza."[25] It reads, "Demonstrations against the Israeli bombardment of Gaza were held in Melbourne, Sydney, Perth, Adelaide, Brisbane and Canberra over the weekend—the second

---

[25] http://www.wsws.org/en/articles/2014/07/21/aint-j21.html 5 Aug 14

round of such protests in Australia's major cities in the past week. Attended by workers and students, including many immigrant and Middle Eastern families, the largest rallies were held in Melbourne, where more than 5,000 participated and in Sydney where over 3,000 attended. Sydney protesters marched down George Street chanting: "In our thousands, in our millions, we are all Palestinian."! Multiculturalism has allowed a diverse number of foreign religions to become firmly established and entrenched here. It has given rise to a controversial 'Political Correctness' that has confused many. Many of the forgoing religions are now energetically spreading their belief systems throughout the land and are seeking to make converts by actively proselytizing and converting people. Those who raise an objection to their activities are immediately branded as being xenophobic, which means to have an intense or irrational dislike, or fear, of people who come from other countries! The foregoing leads to many people now asking new and different questions about the future than they did in times past. To illustrate how confused some people are, I list some of those questions that I've been asked in recent years:

What is the difference between Christianity and Buddhism, we all believe in the same god don't we?; If Islam is a religion of peace, as they keep telling us it is, then why are they always rioting and killing people and fighting among themselves like they do?; Was Islam the reason behind the recent Cronulla riots and the riots in Sydney; Why are so many Australians converting to Eastern religions, like Hinduism, Taoism and Buddhism?; Why are our churches, government agencies and medical profession promoting practices like Meditation and Yoga; What about Martial Arts, is there anything spiritual about it?

From my research I believe that all the foregoing are

steeped in religious beliefs and practices! As a Christian I know that they are not compatible with the true Christian Faith?

It's only natural that the 'frontline people' who represent these new religious groups publicly, have been hand-picked and trained, in how to best 'sell' their belief system to our politically correct media, government and an unsuspecting and naïve public! The training these people have received means they are ready, willing and waiting, to answer any question, or any objection, that might be put to them about their beliefs. They have been taught to do this with in an authoritative, positive and sincere manner. What they want to discuss with you is a very much rehearsed and parroted presentation. For many unsuspecting folk, their responses are deliberately loaded to control your responses and therefore dangerous to your spiritual health!

In most of our communities and schools today, there is a total lack of teaching of any description, which has been designed to assist people to learn how to cope with the pain, suffering and grief that often comes when the death of a loved one occurs. Even the despair some suffer, when they contemplate their own impending death, they find there is there is a lack of truthful counsel and good material available to them. I believe that death is a part of life and it's going to happen to all of us at some time in the future! There should be training available to educate and assist people to deal with it before it becomes a reality, or pending reality, in their own lives and that of their families!

Members of the Jehovah's Witnesses, when I was involved with them back in the 1960's, whom I knew personally, were encouraged and coerced to read their local newspaper's death and funeral notices. This was done in order to ascertain if there were any deceased persons listed who had lived in their 'Congregation's Area of Responsibility'. If there was a deceased one listed, they would establish the address where they lived and then they would go and knock on the doors of all the other homes in their street, or locality, and deliberately miss the home of the deceased! They did this so that they could speak to people, on what was for them a 'convenient' topic to raise about, "Life After Death"! I never took part in this as I felt was a rather macabre activity. They would deliberately ask the neighbours of the deceased, what I would term the loaded, or 'bait question', "Did you hear about the unfortunate death of 'so-and-so'?" Which in most cases would open the discussion and lead them to asking what I term, also loaded, or 'the hook' question, "Where do you think he (or she) is now"!

The writer and the reader both know that one hundred percent of everyone who reads this book will eventually die! I believe that a statistic like that should be sufficient reason, to motivate people to try and learn something about death and dying, don't you? Sadly, most people have absolutely no idea how they should deal with suffering and death whether it comes through age, terminal sickness, or an 'out of the blue' accident?

During a time of grieving for the loss of a loved one, questions about life after death often beset people. Even having a loved one suffering from severe dementia, who no longer recognises them, leads people to have thoughts about death and dying! They may even suffer and grieve for their loved one before they actually died! Dementia was once described to me as being, "…just like a living death"! I know what this insidious disease is like. My father-in-law and then my mother, both suffered from it for many years! With their eventual passing it was as if it was a release from what we had perceived as suffering! Fortunately, both of them were Born-again Christians and we knew that their earthly hope of life in Heaven after their deaths had been fulfilled!

It is things like a terminal illness; a fatal accident or a disabling one; a forced retirement; an unexpected job redundancy; a long-term unemployment period and the like which are all circumstances which are taken advantage of by many of the cult groups! They tend to strike at the very time when people are most vulnerable! Just as there is no provision to learn about death and dying, there is no provision, in our permissive, politically correct and so-called tolerant society, that has been developed to inform and teach people what a false and dangerous religious or a dangerous non-religious cult group looks like!

Remember, information is readily and freely available on the Internet and at your local library! It's not just the 'not knowing' factor which disadvantages most people during times of emotional and physical stress. There is another factor which is scary for some and that is, what I mentioned earlier, the 'spiritual factor'. Whether a person is aware of it or not, there are forces of evil, who see them, when they are down and discouraged, as being prime targets to enslave as members of a religious or non-religious group in order to keep them in bondage and away from the true Gospel of Jesus Christ!

Mature Christians know that the end result of a person's involvement with cults that claim to be 'christian' can lead them into an eternal and Christ-less Eternity! Not only have they become the victims of their own naivety and ignorance, but sadly at times, they have often been helped on their way by seemingly uncaring, indifferent and uninformed church members with the things they say, or don't say, and what they do, or don't do!
It is my belief and fervent hope, that by the time the reader reaches the end of this book that they will be sufficiently equipped with the necessary knowledge to personally stay away from such

dangers. It's my belief also, that they will be equipped sufficiently to teach their loved ones and friends how to become 'cult-proof'!

On the other hand, should the reader come to understand that they and/or their loved ones, are involved with, or being confronted by, or have been befriended by members of a cult group, then I would encourage you to be strong and make every effort to extricate yourself and your loved ones from those contacts as quickly as possible. Be encouraged by the exhortation that Timothy received from the Apostle Paul when he said, *"All Scripture is given by inspiration of God, and is profitable for doctrine (teaching), for reproof, for correction, for instruction in righteousness, that the man (or woman) of God may be complete, thoroughly equipped for every good work."*[26]

By committing oneself to undertaking a carefully directed study of the Scriptures, many parts of which are quoted throughout this work, along with the use of the insights presented, the writer knows that if the reader is, or becomes, a truly Born-again Christian and has made Jesus Christ their personal Lord and Saviour, then their study and prayers will help them and others whom they share with, to grow spiritually. If the reader makes the effort, I know that he, or she, will be richly rewarded. Someone has said, "The Christian life is like a bank, you can only get out of it what you put into it!"

In what way you may ask? Firstly, your study will help you to become more firmly established in your own understanding of the important core teachings of the Bible. Secondly, it will equip and enable you to become firmly planted and established in God's Kingdom. This has the added effect of bringing you to the point

---

[26] 2nd Timothy 3:16-17

where you will no longer be "tossed to and fro and carried about with every wind of doctrine" (or teaching), which tends to 'blow' through the church and our secular society, like a wind, as the writer of Ephesians infers.

In the writing of this book, I believe I am being obedient as one who has been called into the ministry and tasked with the doing the following: *"And He Himself gave some to be apostles, some prophets, some evangelists, and some pastors and teachers, for the equipping of the saints for the work of ministry, for the edifying of the body of Christ, till we all come to the unity of the faith and of the knowledge of the Son of God, to a perfect man, to the measure of the stature of the fullness of Christ; that we should no longer be children, tossed to and fro and carried about with every wind of doctrine, by the trickery of men, in the cunning craftiness of deceitful plotting, but, speaking the truth in love, may grow up in all things into Him who is the head—Christ— from whom the whole body, joined and knit together by what every joint supplies, according to the effective working by which every part does its share, causes growth of the body for the edifying of itself in love.* [27]

It was wise King Solomon who said, *"...there is nothing new under the sun. Is there a thing of which it is said, "See this is new"? It has been already in the ages before us."*[28] Here, the King informs us that there is *"nothing new under the sun"*. Therefore, as the writer of this book, I cannot claim originality for much of the content. It has been learned from my personal life experiences and the concepts and principles which can be found, not only in the Bible, but also in the teachings of knowledgeable and well qualified Christian

---

[27] Ephesians 4:11-16
[28] Ecclesiastes 1:0b-10a

expositors – many of whom are still with us and numerous others who have gone before us in generations past. They were all well experienced in defending the true Christian Faith.

May you find and know God's richest blessing as you read, absorb, and grow in your understanding of just how important it is to know what the Bible, God's Word actually teaches. My prayer and hope is that you will become equipped to handle the Word of God aright in the midst of what today is a veritable 'cult explosion' exploiting what is going on in the church and in our world today!

The Apostle Paul said, *"And what I do I will continue to do, in order to undermine the claim of those who would like to claim that in their boasted mission they work on the same terms as we do. For such men are false apostles, deceitful workmen, disguising themselves as apostles of Christ. And no wonder, for even Satan disguises himself as an angel of light. So it is not strange if his servants also disguise themselves as servants of righteousness. Their end will correspond to their deeds."*

(2ND Corinthians 11:12-15 Revised Standard Version)

CHAPTER TWO

Staying on the Right Track

Since I began to teach the concepts, reveal the facts, and offer the insights which I've recorded in this book, there have been many inquiries from folk, who after reading same, or listening to, or watching our recorded messages, and even after having attended our seminars, have contacted us requesting further help from us after their first contact with a member of a cult! There is absolutely nothing wrong with that, but it soon became apparent to us, that these well-meaning people were all experiencing exactly the same difficulties! When they tried to respond effectively, during their discussions with a member of a cult, it was the questions that the various cult members put to them that they had no answers for! They had simply been 'stumped' by them!

After listening to the details of how they entered into their encounters, it became patently obvious, that in every instance, the difficulties they were experiencing, and were being confronted with, arose simply because, in their view, there seemed to be an inadequacy on their part to respond and answer the cultist's questions? They felt they were not equipped to respond to what was being asked of them about particular teachings and comments that were being asked by the cultist - even after they had read this book! So, what was the problem? Nearly all the enquirers were asking for additional information and extra materials to help them to respond, in their minds refute, what the cultist had challenged them with! They had totally forgotten that it's not about winning an argument, or proving a point, but about planting seeds and winning the person they were speaking with to Christ!

However, the following are just some of the cultist's questions that they were asking us for further information on: should we be celebrating Christmas, Easter and birthdays; should we be observing national holidays; should we allow blood transfusions or an infusion of blood product for a loved one if I'm told they need it; should I be serving in the military actively as I am, or passively by only serving only in the medical corps; should I be eating meat; is the Holy Spirit an 'active force' like electricity;[29] what about those Pentecostal people who speak in 'tongues', are they of the devil; is the Old Testament authentic or is it simply just folklore; has my translation of the Bible been corrupted and is it wrong; should church services be conducted on a Saturday and not on Sunday; what is the 'Mark of the Beast'; what is the number '666' all about; shouldn't there be just one religion on earth that God is using; should we celebrate Communion once a year as Jehovah's Witnesses do; why are there so many different denominations and religions? I could go on but space does not permit.

---

[29] The Holy Spirit is actually the 'Third Person' of the Godhead, or the Trinity! Please read John 14:14-17 and note that the Holy Spirit is referred to by the use of Objective Personal Pronouns, vis., 'He' and 'Him'! Note also that the Holy Spirit is referred to as being, "...another Counsellor" – which an 'active force' could never be!

There have been many and varied requests made to us for extra information over the years – even asking us to come and speak to the cultist for them, which of course we can't do, usually because of the tyranny of distance! I've listed the foregoing questions to illustrate an important point that I wish to make and that is, that in almost every instance, when I asked the enquirer how much time they had spent, during their conversation with the cultist, asking the most important question, "Who do you believe Jesus Christ is?" By their response, we learned that in almost every instance, they had spent no time at all, or very little, pursuing what we believe is the most important question of all! What these people had done was to allow themselves to be diverted into discussing peripheral, or the less important issues!

Keep in mind that the following seven words are the most important words you can ask anyone on this planet, "<u>Who do you believe Jesus Christ is</u>?" In fact, what these well-meaning people had really done was to actually lose control of the conversation and allow themselves to be drawn into discussing topics and issues that have absolutely nothing to do with availing oneself of true Salvation – which of course can only be found by asking for forgiveness of one's sins and for the true Lord Jesus Christ to come into one's life and be their personal Lord and Saviour - and thereby being Born-again! And that is the whole crux of the matter – to help people find and come to know personally the real Lord Jesus Christ! Remember, that if anyone who comes to you from a 'Bible using cult' (notice I didn't say 'Bible believing' cult), wants to raise anything else as an issue, they are simply throwing up a very effective 'smokescreen' which is spiritually designed to keep people from getting to know the true Lord Jesus! Whatever else a cultist may want to talk about with you is really of no importance at all and just a waste of your time. I can only describe a lot of what they say is waffle! We should never make the mistake of playing into the hands of the cultist by discussing their own strange, unique and deviant teachings! Their group's interpretation and understanding of familiar Christian terminology and teachings is quite different and almost always wrong. Their 'teachers' have hijacked and re-interpreted Christian terminology! They may look like genuine Christians and sound like genuine Christians, but they are not!

Never, and I repeat, never should we try to beat, refute, wrangle, or argue on matters that only relate to their false teachings – which, as mentioned, I call the 'peripheral issues'! They are the very questions and issues, being raised by your cultist, which invariably are the same questions and issues that once had them 'baffled' and got them hooked? They sincerely believe their group answered those questions for them, so they joined with them and they are nose using those very same questions and issues, to try to convert you! One of the oldest 'tricks in the book' that cults will use, is to ask a person a question which they probably weren't even remotely thinking about, and then answer it for them from their own false understanding!

It has always been my belief, which has been gained from years of personal experience and the experiences of many other folk who have related to us over the years, that after one establishes in the mind and heart of the person, who has challenged your faith, or maybe the one you have challenged, that in time they will respond and come to know and accept the real Lord Jesus into their lives. It is then and only then, when a person is genuinely Born-again, that the peripheral and non-important issues the individual may have had, will begin to pale into insignificance for them! The reason for this is that the Born-again person can now see for himself just how insignificant and

unimportant those issues really were in the first place. I came to a point where I was able to look back and see just how little bearing, or effect, those issues have on a person's Salvation. Note how the Apostle Paul wrote in his letter to the Colossians in Chapter 1:19 as to who Jesus Christ really is: *"For it pleased the Father that in Him all the fullness (of the Godhead, or Deity) should dwell, and by Him to reconcile all things to Himself, by Him, whether things on earth or things in heaven having made peace through the blood of His cross."* He reinforces this truth again in Verses 2:8-10, *"Beware lest anyone cheat you through philosophy and empty deceit, according to the tradition of men, according to the basic principles of the world, and not according to Christ. For in Him dwells all the fullness of the Godhead bodily; and you are complete in Him, who is the head of all principality and power..."*
(Parenthesis added).
When the truth of Christ's Deity has been established in a person's mind and heart – when you are blessed to get to this stage - there will be very little trouble arising from what were the former controversial 'peripheral issues'. It's always the 'peripheral-issues' which cultists will passionately want to raise with you.

Why should you discipline yourself and learn this type of approach? Because by concentrating and centreing your discussion on Jesus Christ alone and who He really is – He is God manifest in the flesh - then you will be exactly where the Holy Spirit needs you to be! Why do I recommend this approach? Because the Scriptures clearly reveal to us that it is the Holy Spirit's responsibility and ministry to teach people and lead them into all truth! The Apostle John writes of this, when Jesus said,
"These things I have spoken to you while being present with you. But the Helper, the Holy Spirit, whom the Father will send in My name, He will teach you all things, and bring to your remembrance all things that I

said to you. Peace I leave with you, My peace I give to you; not as the world gives do I give to you. Let not your heart be troubled, neither let it be afraid"

By following and sticking to this approach, we have often been able to rejoice at how easy a task we have had of flowing in and with the will of God backed by the ministry of the Holy Spirit. Please remember, it is God's ministry to draw a person to Himself, and not ours, for the Scripture says: *"No one can come to Me unless the Father who sent Me draws him; and I will raise him up at the last day."* And, *""Therefore I have said to you that no one can come to Me unless it has been granted to him by My Father."*[30]

Scripturally, it is the Holy Spirit's ministry to convict a person of his sinful state, in order to assist him to recognize he has a need of a personal Saviour. Then, with the guidance and help of the Holy Spirit, we are tasked to teach and lead them into the deeper truths of the Bible and to ensure they become disciples. Standing with and alongside someone and helping them to learn how to live the Christian life, is what is called 'Disciple Making'. Which is the coaching and mentoring ministry that all Christians are called to be involved in[31] with those who have newly come to accept Jesus Christ as their Lord and Saviour. This is the true Salvation that only He can offer. From our experience, it normally becomes a very simple operation to 'mop up' and clear up the 'issues' that initially may have seemed so important to them. We should never forget that it is the ministry of the Holy Spirit to

---

[30] John 6:44 & 65

[31] Matthew 28:19-20, "Go therefore and make disciples of all the nations, baptizing them in the name of the Father and of the Son and of the Holy Spirit, teaching them to observe all things that I have commanded you; and lo, I am with you always, even to the end of the age."

teach them truth and lead them in their newfound lifestyle!

We need to be always mindful of the fact that when we speak to a person from a cult, that we have actually engaged in a spiritual battle. A battle that is unseen and one that can only be overcome by the power of God through prayer! This is why we need to allow for and to ensure that the Holy Spirit has room to function in his role of bringing people to an understanding of truth. We are simply to act as His agents, or the conduit through whom He can work and minister. Just how important this is, was highlighted by the Lord Jesus himself, when He said: *"Therefore I said to you that you would die in your sins, for if you do not believe that I AM (He* [32]*) you will die in your sins"* [33]

One can rest-assured that the Lord Jesus Christ is none-other than the Great I AM! Yes, Jesus Christ is the same 'I AM' that Moses spoke with when he was summoned to stand before the burning bush, as recorded in Exodus 3:14 which says, *"And God said to Moses, "I AM Who I AM." And He said, "Thus you shall say to the children of Israel, 'I AM has sent me to you."'* All would have to agree that God the Father was speaking with Moses! [See Appendix Two for further Scriptural proof that Jesus is God from both the Old and the New Testaments.]

To establish this most important and major fact in the mind and heart of your hearer should be your goal. Once achieved it is great to have the joy of watching the 'unseen work' of the Holy Spirit bringing about their Salvation! This is one of the most marvelous things I have ever witnessed and for which I am very

---

[32] If your Bible translation uses the word "He" here, then it should be *italicised* as *"He"* because the word is not in the original manuscripts. It was inserted wrongly by the translators.

[33] John 8:24

grateful to be a part! May God richly bless you as you seek to bring to others the real Truth that the Lord Jesus is the only one who can save and grant Eternal Life! Notice what Paul had to say in his letter to the Philippians in Chapter 2:3-11:

"Do nothing out of selfish ambition or vain conceit. Rather, in humility value others above yourselves, not looking to your own interests but each of you to the interests of the others. In your relationships with one another, have the same mindset as Christ Jesus: Who, being in very nature God, did not consider equality with God something to be used to his own advantage; rather, he made himself nothing by taking the very nature of a servant, being made in human likeness. And being found in appearance as a man, he humbled himself by becoming obedient to death— even death on a cross! Therefore God exalted him to the highest place and gave him the name that is above every name, that at the name of Jesus every knee should bow, in heaven and on earth and under the earth, and every tongue acknowledge that Jesus Christ is Lord, to the glory of God the Father."

CHAPTER THREE

Cults, Dead Ends of Deception

There are several explanations for the meaning of the word 'cult'. Here are some. The word is derived from the Latin word 'cultus' which means, 'a system or variety of religious worship'. However, it has been used to refer to, 'any form of worship of an unorthodox religious group; any kind of ritual, ceremony or liturgy'. The word 'cult' was also recently defined by another as being "…a teaching, group or movement, which deviates from orthodoxy while claiming to represent the true faith". The Merriam-Webster Dictionary online site says of the word, "a small religious group that is not part of a larger and more accepted religion and that has beliefs regarded by many people as extreme or dangerous".

Remember that all cults deviate in some way from what is regarded as being orthodox, or conventional, in their faith and practice. A conventional faith conforms to what is has been recognised as following established and acceptable doctrines, or teachings, down through the centuries. True Christianity is for everyone – from those of the highest intellect to the lowest.

Therefore, I believe that a great 'litmus test' to apply when someone has challenged your faith by telling you that you are in the wrong place spiritually, is for you to ask yourself the question, "Is what this person telling me capable of being explained to and understood by an illiterate member of an uneducated remote tribal community?" Why this question? Because if what is being put to you can't be understood by unlearned people, then it is not the true Gospel! The true Gospel, as any reader will know, is capable of being understood and received even by little children!

When confronted by a person who tries to tell you that you are in the wrong place spiritually, it helps if you are able to apply Biblical standards, or rules, in order for you to know if that person comes to you in truth or falsehood. Why? Because there are many similarities between true Christianity and 'false christianity'. The writer believes the latter should simply be called 'religion'. As the reader would be well aware, that throughout history, religion has done absolutely nothing to advance the cause of humanity, nor has it created anything of lasting good! As stated, before, religion is a curse! One only has to look at the turmoil being caused by religion in our world at this very moment! Jesus said: *"For false christs and false prophets will rise and show great signs and wonders to deceive, if possible, even the elect."*[34] The 'elect' referred to here are true Born-again Christians. So, logically, if even a true Christian is in very real danger of being deceived, then how much easier must it be to deceive one who has no spiritual insight and

---

[34] Matthew 24:24

no understanding of the Bible, or what it means to be a Christian? One who has never been exposed to sound Christian teaching is at a disadvantage from the very start!

Satan the Devil – yes, he really does exist - has 'earned' the title of being the 'Father of Lies'. His strategy has always been to frustrate the building of the Kingdom of God by raising up:

<u>False Prophets</u>: In the Gospel of Matthew 7:13-23 he says of these, *"Enter by the narrow gate; for wide is the gate and broad is the way that leads to destruction, and there are many who go in by it. Because narrow is the gate and difficult is the way which leads to life, and there are few who find it. "Beware of false prophets, who come to you in sheep's clothing, but inwardly they are ravenous wolves. You will know them by their fruits. Do men gather grapes from thorn bushes or figs from thistles? Even so, every good tree bears good fruit, but a bad tree bears bad fruit. A good tree cannot bear bad fruit, nor can a bad tree bear good fruit. Every tree that does not bear good fruit is cut down and thrown into the fire. Therefore by their fruits [35]you will know them". "Not everyone who says to me, 'Lord, Lord,' shall enter the kingdom of heaven, but he who does the will of My Father in heaven. Many will say to me in that day, 'Lord, Lord, have we not prophesied in Your name, cast out demons in Your name, and done many wonders in Your name?' And then I will declare to them, 'I never knew you; depart from me, you who practice lawlessness!'*

---

[35] The 'fruits' of a 'false prophet' are false prophecies! Many so-called 'christian cults' have a history of false prophecies that have been covered up and explained away by them – otherwise they, when exposed, are non-events that are nothing more than an embarrassment to them.

False Apostles: The great missionary and church leader the Apostle Paul refers to them, *"But what I do, I will also continue to do, that I may cut off the opportunity from those who desire an opportunity to be regarded just as we are in the things of which they boast. For such are false apostles, deceitful workers, transforming themselves into apostles of Christ".* 2 Corinthians 11:12-13

False Teachers: The works of these ones are exposed by the Apostle Peter in 2nd Peter 2:1-3, *"But there were also false prophets among the people, even as there will be false teachers among you, who will secretly bring in destructive heresies, even denying the Lord who bought them, and bring on themselves swift destruction. And many will follow their destructive ways, because of whom the way of truth will be blasphemed. By covetousness they will exploit you with deceptive words; for a long time their judgment has not been idle, and their destruction does not slumber."*

False Pastors and False Shepherds: Physician, evangelist and Gospel writer Luke in Acts 20:29-30 refers to these, *"For I know this that after my departure savage wolves will come in among you, not sparing the flock. Also from among yourselves men will rise up, speaking perverse things, to draw away the disciples after themselves".*

In basic terms, all those who fall into the foregoing 'categories' are all going to have the outward appearance of being just like one expects Christians to look like, but in reality they are just 'wolves in sheep's clothing'! They will talk like a Christian; behave like a Christian; dress like a Christian, as one would expect! Much of what they will say to you will seem to be what you would expect a Christian to be saying. Do you find this confusing? Well…

Satan's strategy first and foremost is and has always been, to try to confuse people and cause strife when it comes to Christians and Christianity in order to keep people away from the true and living God. The Bible shows repeatedly that Satan the Devil is the instigator and author of both confusion and strife! People who accept the false, or the counterfeit, have placed themselves in very real danger. Even when the truth is presented to them, they will reject it outright! Why? Because the false will always very closely resemble the true and at times even look better! How could this be?

This type of rejection comes only because there is a lack of sound Bible knowledge and spiritual discernment on the part of the individual. Sometimes, even those in Christian ministry, who should know better, frequently reject the truth when it is presented lovingly to them! Sadly, the most confusing thing for most people is that both the 'true faith' and a 'false faith' are very similar in their characteristics. By way of illustration, note the following:

- Both the true and the false will require that their leadership be strong.
- Both the true and the false will fervently stress the need for loyalty and commitment to their leadership.
- Both the true and the false will believe one must also have a deep commitment to the group, its purpose, and its future goals.
- Both the true and the false will share the belief that they are living in the 'End Times', or the 'Last Days', which are referred to in detail in Matthew Chapter 24 and many other places in the Bible.

- Both the true and the false will work tirelessly to establish a hope for a different and better life-style for the future, not only for themselves, but for their families and others.

A good thing to remember is that true leadership will always work under the authority of the Lord Jesus Christ; whereas the false will tolerate and encourage the deification, or the exalting like a god, of their leader, or leaders, even though they may frequently tell them they are under Christ's authority, when they are not.

People of the true faith will always look to the Bible for their instruction and guidance; but the false will invariably have other 'special' and therefore, in their mindset, supposedly more important and up-to-date 'writings' that will embrace material supposedly far superior to, or in addition to the Scriptures.

For example, the Church of Jesus Christ of Latter Day Saints (the 'Mormons') have their Book of Mormon; The Pearl of Great Price; and their voluminous 'Journal of Discourses', and many other books. Jehovah's Witnesses have their Watchtower and Awake Magazines and over the years published a multitude of hardcover books; Seventh-day Adventists have the voluminous and plagiarized writings of their 'messenger' or 'Spirit of Prophecy' and "source of truth" in their Mrs. Ellen G. White. You will always be able to recognise a dangerous religious group by their rejection of one or all of the following points:
- The absolute Authority of the Word of God, the Bible
- The Deity of the Lord Jesus Christ. (The Bible clearly teaches that there is one God who eternally exists in three distinct but coequal persons: The Father, Son, and Holy Spirit).

- The significance and importance of what took place for mankind on the Cross at Calvary, and
- The Blood Atonement which was paid for by the Lord Jesus Christ on the Cross at Calvary.

Dangerous 'christian' religious groups, will always promote the idea among their followers that they alone have 'the truth', or, "the only way' ordained by God. This leads them to seeing every religion other than theirs as being of the Devil, or under his influence. The classic deception, I believe, is that of the Christadelphians[36], who show their contempt for the Scriptures by believing that Satan the devil does not even exist! Groups who do not claim to be 'Christian-based' will always maintain that their 'Way', or 'Pathway to enlightenment' is the only, or best way, to follow for one to be able to achieve things like, ensuring you have a better life next time round. This is a major teaching from the Hindu religion – it's called Reincarnation! The Hindu's goal is to achieve liberation from the endless cycle of birth, life and death.[37] Many seek to escape by obtaining enlightenment and reaching what they call Nirvana.[38] Others are led to believe that they are

---

[36] Christadelphianism teaches the same two lies as literally every cult and false religion: it denies the deity of Jesus Christ and preaches a works-based salvation. Regarding the deity of Christ, Christadelphianism teaches that Jesus was more than a man, but less than God.
More: http://www.gotquestions.org/Christadelphianism.html

[37] *'Samsara'* is the repeating cycle of birth, life and death. Also in Buddhism, Jainism and Taoism. http://people.howstuffworks.com/reincarnation1.htm Accessed 28 May 2014

[38] *'Nirvana'* is a Sanskrit word that literally means "blown out" as in snuffing out a candle. Someone has said that it also means, "to kill oneself off"! The attainment of Nirvana is called *moksha* which Hindu believes is to be liberated

only seeking to simply live a healthier, more fulfilled and better life now and say they are not into the spiritual side!

It is interesting to note, that the famous Indian guru and national leader, Mahatma Gandhi, is on record, as saying of reincarnation that, "...it is too great a burden to bear"! Why? Because he saw the fruits of the practice in his country which contributes to the extreme poverty, hopelessness and abject despair of his people![39] Basically, the Hindu believes that when one dies, one's body decomposes but something of oneself is reborn into another body. It is the belief that one has lived before and will live again in another body after death in this life.

It's only logical that if the leaders and members of these groups hold such 'world views', or 'mindsets', and have compelling charisma, or attractiveness, then they have the potential to lead others to accept their deceitful and false beliefs. Everyone who is not part of their group, is therefore seen as being lost, unenlightened, less than intelligent, the enemy, or as being spiritually deficient in some way! Which naturally leads them to hold a sense of superiority.

For the group, this 'sense of superiority' tends to develop, and produces in them, what often becomes what is referred to as a 'siege mentality'. This means that whenever someone opposes, or exposes them for what they really are, such exposure is often regarded by them as being an attack, being persecuted, or even discriminated against! Cults always reject, or regard as being suspect, all authority other than their own.

---

from the cycle of rebirth and the extinguishing of all desire, aversion and delusion.

[39] http://www.freerepublic.com/focus/news/2454949/posts Accessed 30 Apr 2014

ANSWER TO THE CULT EXPLOSION

To illustrate: The Jehovah's Witnesses have placed themselves above the law of the land when it conflicts with their own ideals, teachings and practices. As all cults that use the Bible usually do, they justify themselves and their actions of defiance against the law, by quoting what we call a 'proof text'! It goes like this; the JW's will use the following Scripture to justify their defiance of any law that conflicts with their teachings and practices: *"...the high priest asked them, saying, "Did we not strictly command you not to teach in this name? And look, you have filled Jerusalem with your doctrine, and intend to bring this Man's blood on us!" But Peter and the other apostles answered and said: "We ought to obey God rather than men".*
The JW's blindly follow orders and adhere to the teachings emanating from their Governing Body[40] of the Watchtower Bible and Tract Society in Warwick, NY, USA, to the letter and without question. This is because they have been taught that the men who make up the 'Governing Body' are the only ones in the world today who are able to hear directly from their 'Jehovah God'! They will do this rather than submit to their local state and federal laws when it conflicts with what they have been taught to do!

To hold to such false teaching allows the leadership, and members of a group, eventually to assume that they are above the law of the land. This 'blind obedience' has had disastrous results, as it did for the JW's in Malawi, in Africa, in the 1960's.

---

[40] The 'Governing Body' is the ruling body of Jehovah's Witnesses and its numbers have varied over the years: From 1974-1980 there were 17 members and as of March 2014 there are only Seven.

This was when thousands of their members were forced to flee across the border for their lives and safety, into other countries. They were seen by other Malawians as being 'unpatriotic', because the JW's were told by their JW leaders to refuse to buy an MCP card, (pictured) for the very small token sum of 50 cents. It was simply a national 'Voter's Registration Card'[41] which granted the bearer the right to vote in elections!

Why did this happen? Because the JW's for decades have been denied, by their leaders, the right to vote in any elections worldwide. They were taught that for them to cast a vote was wrong as it would be a vote for Satan's kingdom! However, the November 1st Watchtower of 1999, decreed that voting was now a matter of conscience – even though the article stated that such a decision should be based on the Jehovah's Witness, "...Bible-trained conscience and his responsibility to God and State"!

This ruling created a further dilemma for the JW's? They have been taught, by their organisation, that they are, "No part of this world and should be neutral in all worldly political affairs"! The JW's are not to swear allegiance to any 'worldly' organisation or nation. They are not allowed to sing a national anthem, or swear allegiance to a nation's leader or flag. Because of this ruling they are not permitted to enlist in a country's armed forces;

---

[41] During the 1960s and 70s Jehovah's Witnesses in Malawi suffered horrible persecution—including rape and murder—at the hands of radical elements associated with the national political party known as the Malawi Congress Party (MCP) under the Kamuzu Banda Regime. During this period the Malawi Constitution made the nation a single-party state, and the MCP constitution explicitly stated that the MCP was the government of the country. That is to say, the Malawi Congress Party and the Malawi government were one and the same.

perform national military service; or be employed in any industry supplying the armed forces. They should not participate in or stand for political office; or participate in any activity associated with proclaiming their allegiance to an 'earthly government'. For many years this has caused untold problems for JW children in schools and for teenagers living in countries where national service in the military is compulsory.

To illustrate how committed the JW's are expected to be in their stance on this, I share the following: In 1968 I was shown a newspaper article about a young JW man in Greece. He had just been released from gaol after having served his third two year gaol term for refusing to serve! The National Service period there was two years. Upon his release from prison, after each two year gaol term, he was immediately called up for National Service again! He was called up a fourth time and again he refused. He was immediately sentenced to another two years in gaol! He was regarded worldwide by the JW's of that time as a being a 'Hero for the faith'. He was held up as an example for all to follow!

"As Christ has a Gospel, Satan has a gospel too; the latter being a clever counterfeit of the former. So closely does the gospel of Satan resemble that which it parades, multitudes of the unsaved are deceived by it." -A.W. Pink

CHAPTER FOUR

Six Cult Danger Signals

In this chapter, I will identify six very clear danger signals that will help and assist one to recognize a dangerous religious group. The list was first published in the book I've already quoted from, 'People's Temple – People's Tomb'. It was one of the first accounts of the Jim Jones mass murder/suicide disaster! When I first read the book, I felt I had to adopt the 'Danger Signals' into our ministry. Because of their importance I repeat them here.

I believe that everyone should learn what each danger signal is and get to know them well. They are great guidelines that will help one to avoid a similar fate to the people of Jonestown and also that which occurred to the followers of the Second Adventism cult known as, 'The Branch Davidians', or 'The Branch'. It was led by one David Koresh and in 1993 at Waco, Texas, USA. The disaster it became is remembered for its armed siege by US authorities that lasted for a long 51 days! It ended with a total of 86 men, women and children losing their lives!

The Six Danger Signals: A dangerous group, religious or not, will always:

1. ABUSE THEIR AUTHORITY – for any group, or church to function effectively and efficiently, members must come under some authority. Cults abuse their authority by gradually 'killing' whatever faith a person may have had in, not only the Bible, but

in their church and even their society.

2.   ABUSE YOUR TIME - cults will try to keep their members in a state of tiredness and exhaustion. They do this by getting them involved in so many meetings and activities that they have little, or no time left to think for themselves. Cults really know how to exploit the fact that tired people are not able to think clearly!

3.   ABUSE YOUR MONEY – cults get their followers giving so much of their money that they and their family end up being deprived, even of the basic necessities of life. This has the effect of keeping members in a state of poverty and in what seems to be an absolute dependence upon the group for even their own sustenance.

4.   ABUSE OF DISCIPLINE - cults will try to keep members living in fear of being chastised, disciplined, or even punished by their leader/s, for the slightest transgression against the group's extremely strict rules and regulations.

5.   ABUSE YOUR SEXUALITY – cults will use, abuse, and even pervert, what is acceptable and natural sexual behavior. They do this in order to keep members in bondage to them. The abuse of sexuality was a major weapon used to control many of the hundreds of people who died at the hands of both Jim Jones and David Koresh.

6.   ABUSE YOUR INTIMACY - cults will attempt to subtly motivate and move their people into a state of isolation from their

non-follower families, their relatives and friends. To do this means that followers become bound to their cause without any influence or distraction from anyone outside the group.

All of the foregoing is accomplished by leading converts to become so involved in attending meetings and being involved in activities that they don't have time for their family, relatives and former friends. They achieve this by establishing in the people's minds what we call a 'siege mentality', of which we referred to earlier, so that all who are not members of the group are therefore logically 'the enemy' and should be avoided at all times – including family!

The writer believes that Satan the devil really 'tipped his hand' so to speak, by revealing his *modus operandi*, or the particular way in which he works or does something, with horrific incidents like Jonestown and the Waco mass-suicide/murder horrors being just two examples! These events, and others like them, stand as grim warnings to all who do not heed Jesus' words in Matthew 7:15, *"Beware of false prophets who come to you in sheep's clothing, but inwardly are ravenous wolves"*...and again in Chapter 24:11, *"Then many false prophets will rise up and deceive many."*

By way of illustration: A sheep, when it is attacked, is no match for a ravenous wolf![42] A wolf can quickly seize, kill, and tear a sheep to pieces! From our verse, and in its context, we can see that the 'ravenous wolves' are representative of the 'false prophets' and the other false offices I have previously mentioned.

The word 'prophet' is simply the name applied to 'one who speaks for another'. In our case this would be for God. In our discussion, and in the context of Scripture, a 'false prophet' is one

---

[42] In Australia our Dingo, or native wild dog, would have the same effect.

who claims to speak for God, but of course, does not! For an example; should a person be on record that on the 30th June 1990 he claimed he had 'a heavenly revelation' and said, "God told me that the world as we know it is going to end on December 31st in the Year 1999". Then prior to and up to the end of December of that year, it could quite correctly be said that they are functioning in the role of "a prophet".

However, with the passage of time – and time as we've said before, is always the enemy of all who prophesy specific dates and events! Time will eventually prove him to be either a true prophet or a false prophet! We all know now that the 'end of the world' did not occur on December 31st 1999 and nothing happened! We all were still here on January 1st in the Year 2000! Therefore, the so-called 'self-proclaimed prophet' has proven to be nothing more than another 'false prophet' and obviously his message did not come from God!

'False Prophets' should not be allowed to explain away their 'failed dates' as being a misunderstanding on their part. Many have lied in the past, saying they did not 'see something else' at the time! Many false prophets have been able to successfully do just that, which allowed them 'off the hook' so to speak![43]

We should always remember, that if the true and living God speaks, then what he says will come to pass. Rest assured when God the Father says something is going to happen, that it will definitely happen! This is because it says in God's Word in Hebrews 6:18 that, *"...it is impossible for God to lie..."* So God will

---

[43] For example, Ellen G. White, the false prophet of the Seventh-Day Adventists and her false 'vision' dates of 1843, 1844 and 1845 for the church to be taken up into Heaven proved false!

never ever say that He is going to do a certain 'thing' at a point in time and then later say that he changed His mind! I'm sorry, there is just one instance that comes to mind. That was when the people of the City of Nineveh repented of their sinful ways, after hearing the word of Jonah, which God gave him to say to them, despite his original disobedience. Jonah was tasked by God to tell them to repent – and they did![44]

Should one choose, or naively follow a proven false prophet – that is a particular person, or an organisation - who is on record as having given and promoted a prophecy, or prophecies, that in time have proven to be false - and abide by their revelations and teachings, it's just as dangerous spiritually for them as it would be for a real sheep to follow after a live ravenous wolf! In Luke 21:8 Jesus said, *"Take heed that you be not misled; for many will come in My name, saying, I AM, and, the time is at hand. DO NOT GO AFTER THEM"*! (Emphasis added).

Many people are simply not aware of God's repeated warnings in His Word the Bible, not to follow dangerous religious groups and believe their wrong interpretations of the Word, nor their heretical teachings. Matthew 24:11 says. *"...many false prophets will rise up and deceive many"*. Verses 23-25 follow saying, *"If anyone says to you, 'look, here is the Christ', or 'There'! do not believe it. For false christs and false prophets will rise and show great signs and wonders to deceive, if possible, even the elect. See, I have told you beforehand"*. (Underlining mine). So, we have no excuse to be caught by a false christ or a false prophet group, because we've been warned. It would indeed be foolish for one to not heed that warning! We should make every effort to become competent and

---

[44] Jonah 1:1-3:10

able to identify dangerous religious and non-religious groups in order to save not only ourselves but our family members too. If we can do that, then we should be able to show others how they can avoid being deceived. We first should 'cult-proof' ourselves, then our family and then our friends. It would be means of great gain as we then would be able to lay hold of true Salvation and have the very real hope of Eternal Life in God's Kingdom and not just wither and die slowly like a cut flower at the end of this life!

The writer would counsel all Christians to resolve to make their church a more loving community towards its members and to all those who visit their services. If you don't make people feel welcome and show them the love of God, you could possibly be contributing to their succumbing to the many 'false gospels' that we have referred to in this work and others we've not mentioned, who function and flourish in our societies today in these difficult and stressful times. To illustrate my point. My wife and I attended a church a few years back, where an elderly couple half-heartedly greeted us at the door when we arrived. After the service had concluded on our first visit, no one came near us to say "Hello"!

The following Sunday, on our second visit, we decided we would make the effort and approach others after the service. People were standing around and sitting in small groups talking. They paid little, or no attention to us, apart from saying 'Hello' when we walked up to them, then they continued with their conversation and completely ignored us! It wasn't until the following Sunday, which was our third, that a person, other than those at the door, came up and introduced themselves to us! That church was definitely not a very friendly or welcoming church – what they had done, without realizing it, was to tell us without words, that we were not really welcome! Is that the way a church should be?

One should personally feel obligated to involve oneself with the job of building meaningful relationships with those in your fellowship and those who visit your church. We should encourage our church members to make themselves available to help the aged, the poor, the sick, the lonely, the unlovely, the underprivileged and the unemployed. Because they are the very people who generally make up most of the vulnerable and needy in our communities and possibly the most receptive to the Gospel.

It's the people in the foregoing categories of society who are particularly vulnerable and at great risk of predatory cult members. People with the greatest needs and hurts have the potential, because of their desperation, of being 'set up' to become cult victims. Even your own children or grandchildren could be at risk? We should all make the effort to help people to know how to recognise a cult and to understand how they operate, even at a very early age. We should never be guilty of doing nothing in this regard because we think they are too young to understand. From an article titled, 'Cult-Proofing Our Kids' the author, one Gretchen Passantino,[45] quotes Matthew 24:23-24 and then says, "Churches with a rigid autocracy teach kids not to think. Kids learn that they're to obey orders without reasons. This kind of environment mimics cults and actually trains kids in the stimulus-response mode of cults-"I command, and you jump!"

She continues, "...parents and churches need to teach kids to think critically about what they believe and why they believe it and how their lives should be ordered according to God's will. We can be so afraid that kids are going to be lured into sin or into false teaching that the church isolates them from any other ideas or

---

[45] http://childrensministry.com/articles/cult-proofing-our-kids/

practices, instead of educating them and giving them good sound answers and choices. The church pretends like those religious choices don't even exist. And then when the kids get out into the world and say, his best friend in school turns out to be a cult member, he's totally unprepared to evaluate what he's hearing or seeing. He really doesn't know how to respond to it."

She then advises that we should, "Love and accept kids unconditionally. If we don't teach children that the church is the place to find God's love and acceptance, cults may convince them (one day) that they are the ones who will love them as God does. (We should) teach kids to understand the Bible. "The focal point for Bible study, for both young children and mature adults, should always ultimately be on the person of Christ."

It only takes just one false prophecy to make one a false prophet.
- Deuteronomy 18:20-22

CHAPTER FIVE

A Word About The Occult

Before proceeding further it would be appropriate and wise, to spend a little time to ensure that the reader does not confuse the 'cults' - with which we are dealing with in this work - with the 'occult'. However, many cults could be described as being 'occultic' in their practices. The word 'occult' is defined in most dictionaries as "…involving anything that is:

> Kept secret or hidden from others
> Clandestine – kept secret especially because it is illicit
> Esoteric - meaning only to be revealed to the initiated; something that is secret, private, even confidential
> Recondite - something that is obscure to the rank and file, or little known to other members
> Something mysterious and beyond the range of ordinary knowledge, or even our human understanding
> Involving supernatural phenomena or influences
> Mystical and veiled
> Magical – the power of apparently influencing events by using mysterious or mystical forces.

The following is a list of names of some of the groups and their practices that would fall into the above categories:-

The Theosophical Society; Spiritualism; Rosicrucianism and its numerous offshoots; The Ordo Templi Orientis (O.T.O.) and its many spin-offs; Gnosis; Alchemy; the Chinese Taoist I-Ching; Sorcery; Freemasonry; Astrology; Numerology; Tarot Cards, Angel Cards, Oracle Cards and Fairy Card readings; After Life Therapy; Divination; Palmistry; and many other forms of esoteric and magical orders too numerous to mention here.

All of the foregoing groups and a multitude of others, along with their practices are collectively known as being involved in 'the occult'. This is because their beliefs, teachings and practices are in most cases kept secret and hidden from the majority of people. Throughout history, the occult, just like the cults, has been present in every generation and just dressed up in different garb. As I said earlier, that there is nothing new about the cults, there is also nothing new about the occult. Unfortunately, the occult has grown like 'a weed in the garden of humankind' for many thousands of years!

The Word of God speaks against such practices, for God sees them all as being loathsome and disgusting, just as Deuteronomy 18:9-13 (RSV) says: *"When you come into the land which the LORD your God gives you, you shall not learn to follow the abominable practices of those nations. 10 There shall not be found among you any one who burns his son or his daughter as an offering, anyone who practices divination (fortune teller), a soothsayer (teller of future events), or an augur (magician), or a sorcerer (witch), 11 or a charmer (hypnotist), or a medium (consulter of spirits), or a wizard (clairvoyant or psychic), or a necromancer (consulter of the dead). 12 For whoever does these things is an abomination to the LORD; and because of these abominable practices the LORD your God is driving them out before you. 13 You shall be blameless before the LORD your God. 14 For these nations, which you are about to dispossess, give heed to soothsayers and to diviners; but as for you, the LORD your God has not allowed you so to do." (Parenthesis added)*

Many people see the occult as nothing more than being delusional and fraudulent and indulged in by nothing but simple-minded people who have been conned by tricksters who are seeking both material and financial gain. It is this sort of attitude no doubt, that causes people to feed off the seemingly harmless stage presentations of magicians and conjurors who employ nothing more than simple sleight-of-hand and cunning concealment. The phenomena resulting from practices in the occult are too well-documented and researched to be dismissed as being simply illusory or imaginary. What may have initially appeared as just being harmless fun, for many, has become devastating and even horrific for having dabbled in and with esoteric occult practices.

For example: Back in the 1950's and 60's, performing under the stage-name *'The Great Franquin'* (Francis Quinn), a New Zealander, became well-known throughout Australia and the world for his amazing ability to hypnotise people. He would have people performing all sorts of bizarre feats on stage at the seeming 'snap of a finger'! After many years he gave up and retired from his stage work. It has been reported that this was after he became aware of how damaging and detrimental to the emotional and behavioral well-being of his 'subjects' were his 'powers' were proving to be with the passage of time!

Today, occult phenomena and secret religions are definitely the 'in-thing' in many societies around the world. There are many New Age stores, complete with their own resident practicing astrologers, palm readers, tarot card readers, fairy oracle and angel card readers etc., who work their craft in them! They have become commonplace in most suburban shopping centres along with their well publicised regional and major city expositions.

In Australia there is an ever increasing tide of the occult filth being foisted upon us, particularly via the film and the periodical magazine industry. In recent years the release of the enormously popular Harry Potter book series and the resulting hit movies are a prime example. Even some of our country's respectable corporate organizations are promoting the occult in their advertising with their use of both occult and astrology symbols. In recent years, many of our major commercial organizations have been promoting the occult in their stores, particularly the Hallowe'en festival[46]! Their sales staff are garbed as witches for the occult observance of Samhain, which is more commonly known as Hallowe'en (also known as All Hallows Eve, All Hallowtide and The Feast of the Dead), which occurs annually every October 31st. When challenged, the organization simply dismissed it as being simply a "popular product promotion"!

The occult holds a tremendous fascination for the uninformed. However, for those who have Jesus Christ as their Lord and Saviour, and who understand and adhere to Christian standards of living, have very little problems with the occult,

---

[46] Each year, on 31 October, an increasing number of witches and wizards darken the doors of Australian households. Halloween was a Celtic festival celebrating summer's end and the coming New Year. In the ninth century, the pagan festival was replaced by All Saints and All Souls Day, when dead souls in purgatory were remembered. On the evening before, All Hallows Eve, the poor would go door-to-door and receive food in exchange for praying for the souls of the dead. In the 19th century, Irish immigrants brought the custom to the United States, where it became an opportunity for revelers to prank their neighbours — the practice of trick-or-treating emerged in an attempt to buy off the pranksters.

because they live in harmony with their Maker's Instructions! Those who are outside of Christ are so often devoid of true peace and happiness, so much so, that they are easily seduced and deceived by the tempting offers made by the occult practitioners to meet and fill what they feel as their perceived needs in their lives.

It is because the occult appears to offer a way in which one can change one's circumstances, or situation for the better, by manipulating or changing their environment, that the unwary are very easily taken-in and deceived. Another reason people become ensnared is because there is always an element of mystery involved with any branch of the occult that people find fascinating and are in awe of. Human nature being what it is, anything that has an 'element of mystery' has its own appeal. This can lure the unwary into becoming involved with the occult. The presence of observable and mysterious phenomena, or signs can appear to validate what is being promoted to them.
It is the case that without Christ in their lives people can often feel that they have no identity, or sense of belonging. This is where the occult seems to again fill a perceived need; by providing an individual with a means of identification in a world of ever increasing anonymity. In our modern societies we have all become just 'a set of numbers' on the computers of a multitude of federal, state, local government and commercial computer systems?).

Here I must inject a warning! Do not be fooled by those who would have you believe that there is a difference between what is termed 'black magic' and 'white magic', or 'black witches' and 'white witches'. There is really no difference! Some will tell you that 'black witches' practice magic for their own purposes, in order to make gain for themselves and to obtain power over people. On the other hand, people will tell you that 'white witches' practice their magic only to help and assist others in need! On the surface this may appear to be a nice thing to do, but the manipulation and control of the individual is still the goal. Remember, the only difference between the two is profit!

Once a person is deceived and ensnared by the occult, they will very soon become involved in religious-type activities or rituals, which all too often have their roots buried deeply in paganism. There is one Internet website which describes and says of their Paganism that it is, "...a religion of nature, in other words Pagans revere Nature. Pagans see the divine as immanent in the whole of life and the universe; in every tree, plant, animal and object, man and woman and in the dark side of life as much as in the light. Pagans live their lives attuned to the cycles of "Nature, the seasons, life and death."[47]

All occult practices are invariably based on certain beliefs, which almost always includes an 'official' organised priesthood and/or leadership. In some groups, they quite unashamedly acknowledge that their source of help comes from none other than a personage named 'Lucifer' – sometimes he is referred to as, The Carrier (or The Bringer) of Light! Christians know this is just another name for Satan the Devil, in spite of the protestations of the occultist. Many occult practitioners will strongly deny that there is even such a being as the Devil!

Therefore, the occult I believe, without any doubt, is used by Satan to confuse and to replace that which God offers mankind freely. Remember, as we discussed earlier, that *"All Scripture is given by inspiration of God, and is profitable for doctrine, for reproof,*

---

[47] From the Website: isle-of-avalon.com/pagan.htm

for correction, for instruction in righteousness, that the man of God may be complete, thoroughly equipped for every good work". (2nd Timothy 3:16-17).

We should all heed the warning given in 1st Timothy 4:1-3, *"Now the Spirit expressly says that in latter times some will depart from the faith, giving heed to deceiving spirits and doctrines of demons, speaking lies in hypocrisy, having their own conscience seared with a hot iron, forbidding to marry, and commanding to abstain from foods which God created to be received with thanksgiving by those who believe and know the truth".*

Dabbling with the occult in any shape or form can be highly dangerous. It can even bring about and cause your demise! Even if it does not do so in this life, then most assuredly it can cause you to miss out on the Good Life in the next! The primary danger of the occult is that it is a path away from God that can bring you into contact with the demonic realm. The demonic forces are tasked to deceive and destroy individuals. Therefore, contact with the demonic breeds numerous problems. In an article written by Patrick Zukeran[48] he states that there are three things about the occult to watch out for:

"Firstly, cult experts and psychologists have documented the connection between occult involvement and psychological and emotional disorders. Participants spend numerous hours studying, practicing, and playing games that involve conjuring demons, sacrificing creatures in cruel rituals, controlling sinister forces, and casting spells to disable and kill their enemies. This can affect a person's spiritual, mental, and emotional state.

---

[48] The World of the Occult : A Christian Worldview Perspective from the Probe Ministries website: http://www.probe.org

"Secondly, there is the danger of spirit possession. The occult arts often require one to empty one's mind and invite foreign spirits to control his or her intellect and body. For example, when operating a *Ouija Board*,[49] participants are asked to empty their minds to allow other forces to guide them as they attempt to obtain spelt-out messages. In other games, participants are encouraged to call upon a spirit being to help guide them. These techniques can open the door for spirit possession.

"Thirdly, there is the danger of violence to oneself and others. Many cases of violence and suicides are connected to the occult. Dr. Thomas Redecki, psychiatrist and chairman of the National Coalition on Television Violence, has given expert testimony at a number of murder trials that were connected to fantasy role-playing games. He states, "I've found multiple instances of attitudes, values and perceptions of reality that were strongly influenced by an immersion in these games. When someone spends 15 to 30 hours a week dreaming of how to go out and kill your opponents and steal treasure, it's not surprising that the desire to act it out in real life occurs... (In conclusion, he says,) Only Christians who come in the authority of Christ can engage the world of the occult and those protected by His armor can resist the Adversary and be delivered from the occult."

---

[49] The Ouija board, also known as a spirit board or talking board, is a flat board marked with the letters of the alphabet, the numbers 0–9, the words "yes", "no", "hello" (occasionally), and "goodbye", along with various symbols and graphics. It uses a planchette (small heart-shaped piece of wood or plastic) as a movable indicator to indicate the spirit's message by spelling it out on the board during a séance. Participants place their fingers on the planchette, and it is moved about the board to spell out words.

Three Scripture Warnings About the Occult

1. "And the person who turns to mediums and familiar spirits, to prostitute himself with them, I will set My face against that person and cut him off from his people." Leviticus 20:6

2. "And when they say to you, "Seek those who are mediums and wizards, who whisper and mutter," should not a people seek their God? Should they seek the dead on behalf of the living? Isaiah 8:19

3. "For the idols[a] speak delusion;
The diviners envision lies,
And tell false dreams;
They comfort in vain.
Therefore the people wend their way like sheep; They are in trouble because there is no shepherd." Zechariah 10:2

"False religions and the occult are closely related. They both seem to promise things that appeal to us: knowledge, power, peace, access to God. Hallucinogenic drugs promise similar 'highs', and there are many other doors also that lead into the realm of the supernatural. All claim to direct us to the light, but in reality every one of them tragically only entices us into spiritual darkness."
-Michael Smith (Source unknown)

CHAPTER SIX

Is There Another Jesus?

IT has been said, "...because cultic groups deviate from the written Word of God (the Bible), they do not accept the Living Word, the Lord Jesus Christ, as being the completely unique Son of God". This statement, as I said earlier, is the crux of the whole matter! All dangerous religious cults who claim to be Christian will in some way deny that Jesus Christ was God manifest in human form. Again, the most important question for you to have answered, when dealing with a member of a cult is, "Who do you believe Jesus Christ is?"

The Apostle Paul warned about those who would preach "...another Jesus than the one we preached" (2nd Corinthians 11:4). He made it quite clear that the preaching of 'another Jesus' was inspired by 'a different spirit' than God's Holy Spirit, and therefore would be promoting a 'different gospel' from the one that was "...once for all delivered to the saints" (Jude 3).

To avoid confusion and to make sure the reader is able to discern the real Lord Jesus Christ from the false, remember that the true Jesus is the founder and central figure of Christianity. He is said to have lived in Palestine from about 5-4 BC until AD 33 (or possibly AD 30?). The name 'Jesus' corresponds with the

Hebrew word '*Yehoshua*' which means 'Yahweh (pronounced "yahway") is Salvation'. Thus the Hebrew letters 'YHWH'[50] represents the more correct name for God the Father (written Biblical Hebrew does not insert vowels and only uses consonants – the reader has to insert the vowels as he reads the text). So, at the risk of upsetting some of my readers, the commonly used name '*Jehovah*' means absolutely nothing at all in the Hebrew language! The name has only been known from about the 14th Century. There is no 'J' or 'W' in the Hebrew alphabet!

Even the Jehovah's Witnesses, who place so much emphasis on the word *Jehovah*', readily admit this fact in the concluding comments of their Foreword in one of their own books.[51] After they have spent the previous 12 pages supposedly proving that God's Name is *Jehovah*' they conclude by saying, *"While inclining to view the pronunciation "Yah-weh" as the more correct way, we have retained the form "Jehovah" because of people's familiarity with is since the 14th century."!*

Christianity was founded on the belief that Jesus is the Messiah, or the Christ, who was promised right through the Old Testament. He came and died to redeem the life that Adam lost and to save mankind from the penalty of their sins. Even ancient non-Christian sources corroborate historical facts about Christ's life and ministry activities.

By far the oldest and more accurate historical information is found in the New Testament Gospels. Attempts have been

---

[50] 'YHWH' is known as the 'Tetragrammaton' which is derived from the Greek word τετραγράμματον, meaning 'four letters' and is the Hebrew theonym יהוה, commonly transliterated into Latin letters as YHWH.

[51] 'The Kingdom Interlinear Translation of the Greek Scriptures' Watch Tower Bible & Tract Society of Pennsylvania, First Edition, 1969, page 23

made by 'liberal Christianity', the New-Agers, various cults, and many other false religions to present Jesus as being just another 'great teacher' or 'a prophet for his time whose ministry and life was radically different from the Biblical historical accounts'. While these efforts often define a 'jesus' who is compatible with their world view, they lack early supporting historical documentation and are thus arbitrary (based on random choice or personal whim, rather than any reason or system) and subjective.

"Reliable sources support the historic, traditional Christian belief that Jesus is the Second Person of the Trinity, in that he was and is fully God and fully man; he was born of a virgin and died on the cross of Calvary as a substitutionary atonement (or sacrifice) for our sins, and he rose bodily from the dead."[52]

Following are just a few representative quotations from various groups that the writer considers to be cultic. The quotations clearly reveal that the "jesus of the cults" is not the Jesus of the Bible!

The Latter-day Saint's 'jesus'

The Church of Jesus Christ of Latter Day Saints, or the Mormons as they are more informally known, claim that Jesus was a "pre-existent spirit who was the brother of the devil"[53] and was married to both Mary and Martha! On March 18, 1855 Mormon Apostle Orson Hyde said: "I discover that some of the Eastern papers represent me as a great blasphemer, because I said, in my lecture on Marriage, at our last Conference, that Jesus Christ was married

---

[52] Quoted from the Watchman Expositor website:
[53] Pearl of Great Price, Book of Moses, Chapter 4:1-4

at Cana of Galilee, that Mary, Martha, and others were his wives, and that he begat children".[54] This, it is claimed, was so that Jesus could "see his seed" before he died at his crucifixion!

Therefore, the Mormon 'jesus' is one whose blood was shed on Calvary and it was not the all-sufficient basis for the forgiveness of man's sins! As a result, one has no option to conclude that the Mormon 'jesus' is not the Jesus of the Bible and is therefore an inadequate saviour for them!

As an aside, the word 'Mormon' is a term originally applied by others to the Latter Day Saints, which they today find somewhat objectionable. This could be for two reasons: firstly, the name 'Mormon' derives from the Greek word '*Mormo*' and relates to both a minor Greek spirit that is said to be a companion of *Hecate* the Goddess of magic and sorcery [who bit naughty children in order to frighten them and to keep them from misbehaving!] and as some say, this is the name by which the 'true god of Mormonism' is known.

The Seventh-Day Adventist (SDA) 'jesus': In the SDA book named, "28 Fundamental Beliefs"[55] In Belief Number 18 it states, "One of the gifts of the Holy Spirit is prophecy. <u>This gift is an identifying mark of the remnant church and was manifested in the</u>

---

[54] Journal of Discourses 2:210

[55]:See:
http://www.adventist.org/fileadmin/adventist.org/files/articles/official-statements/28Beliefs-English.pdf In the Introduction it is claimed, "These statements are made collectively by a group of scholars studying and prayerfully searching the Bible with the help of the Holy Spirit" Therefore they are claiming 'Heavenly Revelation"! Copied 3 Sep 2014

ministry of <u>*Ellen. G. White*. *As the Lord's messenger, her writings are a continuing and authoritative **source of truth** which provide for the church comfort, guidance, instruction, and correction*</u>". They also make clear that the Bible is the standard by which all teaching and experience must be tested."(!) In Ellen G. White's writings she asserts that Jesus Christ was the Archangel Michael. Note the Ellen G. White Estate quote: "Both Ellen White and many non-Adventist Bible scholars equate Michael with Christ. This view does not require any lessening of Christ's full deity"[56].

The Jehovah's Witness 'jesus'

The 'jesus' of the Watchtower Bible and Tract Society, the organization that spawned Jehovah's Witnesses, is said to be the first of created beings but was not the eternally pre-existent member of the Godhead, or Trinity as true Christians believe,(the Jehovah's Witnesses do not believe in the Trinity). Just two quotes from their official JW publications are worth noting:

1) "Our redeemer existed as a spirit before he was made flesh and dwelt amongst men. At that time, as well as subsequently, he was properly known as 'a god' - a mighty One." (Studies in Scripture, Vol. 5, p55).

---

[56]This statement shows how confused the Seventh-Day Adventists are regarding who Jesus really is? On the one hand their 'prophet' says he was Michael and on the other hand they now say they believe in His 'Deity'? So, who's right – their 'source of truth' or today's leaders? Sighted statement made in June 1999 on http://www.whiteestate.org/issues/video.html

2) "...The true Scriptures speak of God's Son, the Word, as 'a god'. He is a 'mighty god', but not 'the Almighty God', who is Jehovah (Isaiah 9:6)".[57] We have to also conclude that the 'jesus' of the Jehovah's Witnesses is not the Jesus of the Bible and therefore is also an inadequate saviour!

The Divine Life Society Integral Yoga Institute 'jesus'

"Remember that Christ is not a person, It's an experience- Christhood. Like Nirvana or Buddha. It's an experience..."[58]

The Christian Science 'jesus'

Mary Baker Eddy, the founder of Christian Science (someone said it is not Christian and is definitely not scientific!) not only rejected the Trinity as being a "heathen belief" (Science and Health, p12) but presented a Jesus typical of Judaism, or Unitarianism: "The Christian who believes in the first commandment is a monotheist. Thus he virtually unites with the Jews' belief in one God and recognizes that <u>Jesus Christ is not God</u> as Jesus Himself declared, but is the Son of God" (Science and Health, p361 – (Underlining mine). Again, this is not the Jesus of the Bible and cannot be an adequate saviour for mankind either!

Agni Yoga Fellowship 'jesus'

'Agni' means 'fire' in Sanskrit. Founded by Russian Nicholas

---

[57] Book 'The Truth Shall Make You Free', Watchtower Bible and Tract Society, 1943 page 47.
[58] 'Satchinananda speaks' p.47-48 June 17, 1975

Roerich and his wife in 1920. It is spiritually based on the teachings of one 'Master Morya', the guru of Helen Blavatsky, founder of the occult Theosophical Society. Note the following, "What is Christ? St. Simeon their 'new' theologian wrote, 'I move my hand, and Christ moves, who is my hand?" [59]

The Way International 'jesus'

What Victor Paul Wierwille (1916-1985), the founder of the 'The Way International',[60] which has suffered several splits over the years, taught about Jesus is succinctly summed up by the title of one of his books, on this very subject, which he titled, 'Jesus Christ Is Not God'![61] He wrote, "Jesus Christ was not with God in the beginning ...The Son of God is not co-eternal (with God) ... If Jesus Christ is God and not the Son of God, we have not yet been redeemed". Just like Christian Science's Mary Baker Eddy, Wierwille said this doctrine of the deity of Christ and the Trinity is a hold-over from paganism and is not a biblical truth! Yes, you've guessed it, the wrong 'jesus' yet again!

The Sun Myung Moon 'jesus'

This so-called 'Korean Messiah' founded the World Unification Church in 1954 (its official name: The Holy Spirit Association for

---

[59] Swami Kriyananda, Eastern Thoughts, Western Thoughts (Nevada City, CA: Ananda Publications, 1975), pp. 67-68.

[60] I mention this group because I had a son-in-law who was once influenced by this group. Over time he proved to have some serious misunderstandings about the Bible and the Church.

[61] New Knoxville. Ohio: American Christian. 1975.

the Unification of World Christianity), known commonly as the in-famous group called the 'Moonies'. In 1984, Moon was convicted of tax evasion in the US and gaoled for a period of 13 months. He also attacks the uniqueness of Jesus. In order to strengthen his own position, he wrote: "Jesus, on earth was a man no different from us except for the fact that he was without original sin...He can by no means be God Himself" (Divine Principles, 1957 pp211, 212). Yes, yet another wrong 'jesus'!

The Transcendental Meditation (TM) 'jesus'

The TM leader, Maharishi Mahesh Yogi, mentioned earlier, received worldwide publicity when the not only the pop-groups, *The Beatles*, but also *The Beach Boys* and many others who were at the peak of their notoriety in the 60's and 70's acknowledged him as their 'spiritual guide'. He shows that he does not understand at all the Jesus of the Bible, by his making the following statement: "I don't think Christ ever suffered or Christ could suffer ... the message of Christ has been the message of bliss"! He too is wrong about the Lord Jesus Christ!

The Hare Krishna 'jesus'

Devotees, or followers, are taught that the "Lord Jesus is the Son of the Supreme Absolute Truth. And Krishna is the Father. He is the Source. Krishna says, "I am the source of everything. From me the entire creation flows. Knowing this, the wise worship me with all their hearts. So Krishna is the Supreme Father, and every other living entity is his part and parcel, or his son."[62] Sadly, another false christ!

A Course in Miracles- (Helen Schucman[63]) 'jesus'

"Jesus is a man, who is like all other men, and the Christ idea, which all men possess and must eventually (be) demonstrated. He becomes the pattern for all of us. Jesus the man was used by the Christ to demonstrate the illusion of the world."...Jesus became what all of you must be. ...Is he the Christ? O yes, along with you. ...Is he God's only Helper? No, indeed. For Christ takes many forms with different names..." (pp. 83-84)."The Son of God ... is not Jesus but our combined Christ consciousness. . ."The name Jesus refers to one who was a man but who saw the face of Christ in all his brothers...so he became identified with Christ, a man no longer at one with God."

The Guru Maharaj Ji 'jesus'

Another Indian Hindu guru. He was known only as Maharaj Ji and was born Prem Pal Songh Rawat, whose Divine Light Mission (DLM) was introduced to the West in 1971. DLM was to be 'de-Indianised' from 1974 and the name was eventually changed to Elan Vital (French for 'life force'). He saw Jesus as being, "...one of the many manifestations of the Godhead", but is not the unique

---

[62] 'The Strange World of the Hare Krishnas' by Faye Levine, Fawcett Gold Medal Book, 1974 p102

[63] Helen Cohn Schucman was an American clinical and research psychologist from New York City. She was a professor of medical psychology at Columbia University in New York from 1958 until her retirement in 1976

manifestation of God as the Bible declares: "So Jesus is living, right! Jesus is living, Ram is living now, Krishna is living now, Buddha is living now, but they have all been united into one very powerful power. And when this power spreads its hand...all the things that are going on wrong in this world are going to be abolished."[64] Another spiritual leader who has the wrong 'jesus'!

Christology, which is the study of the doctrine, or the teaching of the Person, Nature and Work of Christ as God the Son, is where all the 'christian cults' and many false religions deviate from true Historic Christianity. It is their most blatant, obvious and most deadly error! This is why the writer majors on this area of teaching and it alone initially, when he is confronted by, or is confronting a member of a cult!

Remember, a person may be right on every other point of their theology and practice, but if they are wrong on this one, and have taken on board a wrong, or false 'jesus' then they have lost their soul for all eternity! Cults who claim to be Christian (there are those who don't) are usually anti-Trinitarian, and therefore, do not accept the Holy Spirit as being a co-equal member of the Triune Godhead. Some go to great lengths to explain that the Holy Spirit is just an impersonal 'force' which emanates from God to achieve his purposes; or, as some believe, just a 'divine influence'; or 'a spiritual enablement from God'. All of which are totally false assumptions on their part.

Christian author Dave Hunt, writing of the God of Abraham, Isaac and Jacob (God changed Jacob's name to 'Israel'), had this to say, "...At Armageddon, when Yahweh comes to the rescue He reveals Himself as the One whom Israel has pierced!

---

[64] Divine Light Magazine, 1972

Pierced?! When and how could Israel pierce the One who told Moses, "there shall no man see me, and live" (Exodus 33:20)? God, being a "Spirit" (John 4:24), cannot be pierced – but the Messiah coming as a man could be. Jesus, who fulfilled every Messianic prophecy, was pierced on the cross. Why was He crucified? For claiming to be God (John 10:30-33)! Yahweh is speaking in the first person; yet two persons seem to be involved: *"...they shall look upon me whom they have pierced, and they shall mourn for him..."* This 'him' refers to another person - and yet He must also be Yahweh! Therefore, is Yahweh two persons? In fact, He declares Himself to be three in one! Consider this: *"I have not spoken in secret from the beginning; from the time that it was, I was there. And now the Lord God and His Spirit have sent me."* (Isaiah 48:16). Surely the one speaking must be God because He has been speaking from the very beginning. Yet He adds, *"The Lord God, and His Spirit, hath sent me."* Here we encounter God, the Lord God, and the Spirit of God. Could this be what the Holy Spirit inspired the Apostle John to write, in John Chapter 1:1 *"In the beginning was the Word, and the Word was with God, and the Word was God"*?

Surely this One called the 'Word', who existed from the beginning, and is God, must be the same God to whom Isaiah refers as speaking from the beginning. But, the similarities of these two verses don't end there. Both raise almost identical questions. In Isaiah, how can God be sent by God; and in John, how can God be with God? There is only one solution: the Messiah must be God. When Jesus said, *"I and my Father are one"* (John 10:30), the Jews accused Him of blasphemy. When they picked up stones to stone him, Jesus asked why they wanted to kill Him? Their instant reply was, *"...for blasphemy, and because You being a Man, make yourself God"* (Verses 31-33). For the Messiah to declare His deity was the ultimate heresy for the Jews, and therefore the believed he was worthy of being put to death!

According to the Hebrew prophets, the Messiah had to be God and at the same time, the Son of God. If God has a Son, who Himself is God and is one with His Father, that would dissolve the Rabbi's objections. We encounter God's Son a number of times in the Hebrew Scriptures. Speaking prophetically, the Psalmist presents God as declaring one who is to come, *"Thou art my Son; this day have I begotten thee"* (Psalm 2:7). Jehovah's Witnesses and others who deny Christ's deity take this as referring to Christ's birth on earth as the beginning of His existence. That cannot be the case, however, because God speaks of His Son as already existing and warns a God-defying world, *"Kiss the Son, and lest He be angry, and you perish in the way...Blessed are all they that put their trust in him"* (v12).

That the Son of God already existed before His incarnation is clear from a number of other statements by the Hebrew prophets. Solomon quotes the prophet Agur asking, *"Who hath ascended up into heaven, or descended? Who hath gathered the wind in his fists? Who hath bound the waters in a garment?"* The obvious answer is "God". Then he asks, *"what is his son's name..."* (Proverbs 30:4), proving that the Son of God already existed at that time. Shadrach, Meshach, and Abednego were cast into a huge furnace so hot that the flames killed those who threw them in! King Nebuchadnezzar was astonished to see these three Hebrews walking alive in the flames, but then he observes another with them and in wonder exclaims, *"...the fourth is like the Son of God"* (Daniel 3:25).

While promising salvation through the coming Messiah, Yahweh repeatedly declared that He himself was the only Saviour: *"I, even I, am the Lord; and beside me there is no saviour"* (Isaiah 43:11);

"*Look unto me, and be ye saved, all the ends of the earth; for I am God, and there is no one else*" (Isaiah 45:22). And yet this salvation goes to "the ends of the earth" by another who must Himself be God and Messiah; *"I will also give You as a light to the Gentiles, That You should be My salvation to the ends of the earth."* (Isaiah 49:6). God speaks here of Jesus.

Unquestionably, the Hebrew prophets all agree that God exists as a tri-unity; three persons, Father, Son, and Holy Spirit, but still one God and in the Messiah He becomes man without ceasing to be God. Christ's claims that He was God and Man, and one with His Father, agree with the prophets. For Isaiah declared, *"For unto us a child is born..."* (Isaiah 9:6). This refers to His humanity, derived, as foretold, from His virgin mother Mary; the "seed" of the woman of Genesis 3:15. Isaiah then adds, *"For unto us a child is born, unto us a Son is given; and the government shall be upon his shoulder. Of the increase of his government and peace there will be no end, upon the throne of David and over His kingdom, To order it and establish it with judgment and justice, from that time forward, even forever."* (Isaiah 9:6-7).

It is obvious the Son given must be the already-existing Son of God, and He is the Messiah because He will rule on David's throne. Note that Isaiah wrote that the Messiah is God, for he wrote, *"His name is "Wonderful, Counselor, The mighty God."* Therefore, Jesus is, "The Everlasting Father." Here is the same mystery: God is both Father and Son - and only He alone is the Messiah!"

> *"La plus belle des ruses du diable est de vous persuader qu'il n'existe pas."*

"The devil's finest trick is to persuade you that he does not exist."
— Charles Baudelaire, French Poet 1821-1867

CHAPTER SEVEN

ABOUT CULT LEADERSHIP

As mentioned previously, religious cults will always have some extra-Biblical figurehead that becomes for them their 'messiah' or 'christ substitute'. They will invariably accept such a leader without any argument or question as to their particular 'interpretation' of the Bible and their personal 'world view'. The following points are also worth remembering:

People who start cults are usually people who possess great personal magnetism and charisma. They seem to have the unusual ability to attract and inspire followers and generate (or perhaps coerce is the better word?) people into offering great personal zeal, unquestioning dedication and obedience and sadly, even prepared to sacrifice for the cause. Most of these leaders are usually people who manifest giant egos, have great ambitions, and often suffer from what has been termed by some as a 'messianic complex'.

Such leaders will normally base his authority on some 'further' or 'additional revelation' which they credit with personally having received instructions from 'god', or some 'angelic being', or from so-called 'years of conducting a personal in-depth search or study'. These so-called 'revelations' often prove to be 'progressive'. In other words, he or she may add to, or subtract from what they initially said as time goes by, to suit their changing circumstances, or whims, when situations or circumstance may seem to change for them, or are about to. With a little research, one all too often finds that these so-called 'revelations' tend to be often contradictory! The most recent 'revelations' will sometimes completely supersede earlier ones, in order to fit a recent embarrassing development.

For example, Joseph Smith Junior of Mormonism, Ellen G. White of Seventh-Day Adventism and Charles Taze Russell of Jehovah's Witness, are all good examples of false prophets who have been forced to make their contradictory revelations 'progressive' so as to conveniently escape from difficult situations that arose, or had arisen in the past, when their previous predictions looked like failing or had failed already! They had to 'save face' by covering up their known false prophecies from the past that had failed outcomes and had become false predictions.

Invariably, one finds that a particular group started with some authoritarian pronouncement by its founder, which is often claimed as the result of a revelation from God which was received during a period of retreat ('caves' in mountains are very common!) where they claim to have prayed and fasted, or copiously read the Bible, or other 'sacred' writings over many years. These leaders usually emerge from such periods of contemplation proclaiming that, "The Lord Jesus (or God, or an angel) came and revealed himself to me and he told me…"? Victor Paul Wierwille (died in 1985), the founder and then president of 'The Way International' whom I mentioned earlier, is a prime example of this sort of conduct. He reported his so-called revelation from God this way: "I was praying…and that's when he (God) spoke to me audibly, just like I'm talking to you now. He said he would teach me the word as it has not been known since the first century if I would teach it to others" (parenthesis mine).

The Moonies 'Reverend' Sun Myung Moon from Korea also claimed that Jesus appeared to him back in 1936 when he was aged 15. He claimed he was commissioned to be the 'Latter-day Prophet to the world'![65]

[Warning: In case the person reading this may feel that they have been given a revelation similar to the foregoing, the writer strongly recommends that you have it checked out with a mature Christian leader. The Bible cautions us to seek wise counsel on difficult matters. Note what is says in Proverbs 11:14, *"Where there is no counsel, the people fall; But in the multitude of counselors there is safety"*!]

As you can see these cult founders and leaders have not been commissioned, or even 'sent out' by any recognized legitimate, orthodox, Biblically-based denomination or organization! However, the Apostles Paul and Barnabas, were sent out by the Eldership of the Church at Antioch. Please note how it was done correctly from Scripture and recorded in Acts 13:1-3 *"Now in the church that was at Antioch there were certain prophets and teachers: Barnabas, Simeon who was called Niger, Lucius of Cyrene, Manaen who had been brought up with Herod the tetrarch, and Saul*

---

[65] He even claimed he was guided directly by Abraham, Moses, Jesus, Mohammed, Buddha and other saints and sages of all faiths. The official website accessed on 1 May 2014, states, "Sun Myung Moon ceaselessly studied the Bible and other religious teachings in order to unravel these mysteries of life and human history. During this time, he went into deep communion with God and entered the vast battlefield of the spirit and flesh." (http:www.reverendsumyungmoon.org/rev_moon_life.html)

(Paul). As they ministered to the Lord and fasted, the Holy Spirit said, "Now separate to Me Barnabas and Saul for the work to which I have called them." Then, having fasted and prayed, and laid hands on them, they sent them away" (Parenthesis added).

Both men were named among those who were called to be 'prophets and teachers' in the early church. Therefore, it was the eldership, or mature leaders of the church, who recognised their ministry gifts and released them into their mission. Notice they did not appoint themselves as cult leaders do! Barnabas and Paul were 'teaching elders' and only became 'apostles' when they were sent out by the church leaders. By definition, the word *apostle* refers to a person who is 'a sent out one to be a messenger of God'.

Nowadays, there are many so-called 'latter-day apostles and prophets' with dubious qualifications and suspect associations with those of the cults who simply go out to the unsuspecting on nothing but their own authority! This constitutes nothing other than self-appointment! They have not been validated in their assumed office by responsible members of a Holy Spirit guided body of elders, or the leadership of a recognised denomination.

In most cases, since these so-called 'apostles and prophets' are appointed by their own authority, or those whom they frequent with, they are invariably the founders and leaders of their own little group! They are revered by their followers and they alone are solely responsible for all the decision-making within their group, particularly when it comes to financial matters! The resulting effect on the followers of such groups is that, in most instances, have appointed their leaders themselves to 'think for' them.

Such leaders are above question and are accountable to no one but themselves. Dare to challenge them on doctrine or practice and they will respond, *"Do not touch My anointed ones"!*[66] These leaders are followed with blind allegiance and obedience, because the followers have been told exactly what they should do and what they are to believe. Readers who have had contact with members of any one of the cults will very soon realize that the group's followers do not think for themselves. They simply parrot their leader's beliefs and teachings to anyone who will listen to them.

As said before, instant and unquestioning obedience to the leader is an absolute imperative for a cult member! Sun Myung Moon told his followers in several of his speeches and publications, "I will conquer and subjugate the world. I am your brain. The time will come, without my seeking it, when my words will almost serve as law. If I ask a certain thing, it will be done. If I don't want something, it will not be done"![67]

Once a person commits himself to a cultic group he very soon develops a haughty and sometimes cynical attitude, coupled with an almost complete closed-mindedness to any other opinion, Scriptural interpretation, or writing. The effect of this is that most cult followers are not interested in pursuing a rational, intellectual, cognitive evaluation of the facts of a matter.

The writer has often found that within these groups there is usually, for the want of better terminology, a gap, or lack of knowledge between the group's 'inner circle' of leadership and the

---

[66] A misquote of two Scriptures: 1 Chronicles 16:22 and Psalms 105:15, which both say, *""Do not touch My anointed ones, And do My prophets no harm."* In both verses, God is referring to His 'anointed ones' of Old Testament times, the Kings and Prophets and saying not to do them physical harm!

[67] Harry V. Martin and David Caul, Napa Sentinel, March 27, 1992.

one who joins and becomes a new member. This is a very esoteric (means: 'designed for or understood by the specially initiated alone') approach and such 'gaps' exist in groups like Jehovah's Witnesses, Transcendental Meditation, Mormonism, The Way and many others, both religious and non.

The leadership of a cult group is usually very tightly controlled by one man, or one woman, who are invariably backed by an elite 'inner core' of their most 'trusted followers' – who are often called 'elders' but usually are just plain old, "Yes Men" and "Yes Women" whose decisions and actions are very often cloaked in a veil of mystery and aloofness from the general membership.

Cult leaders often live in the lap of luxury, while the ordinary members live a rather bland and austere life of self-denial. This sometimes leads to openly begging, peddling artifacts or selling their group's books and magazines, all to support the extravagant and wealthy lifestyles of their leaders!

As a prime example of how materialistic cult leaders can be, we refer again to 'Osho' the now deceased Hindu Indian guru Bhagwan Shree Rajneesh! Also, the Maharishi Mahesh Yogi (1918-2008) is yet another example. 'Timesonline' says of him, "He sprang to global attention when the Fab Four (The Beatles) meditated with him at his ashram in Rishikesh in February 1968.

The most tangible result was the Beatles' patchy White Album. Undaunted, he set up numerous centres worldwide promoting his Transcendental Meditation (TM) method. "If enough people in an area meditate twice a day for 20 minutes" he said, "crime and ill-health would go down..." (But,) The Natural Law Party, his political wing and his 'yogic flying' do not enjoy such credibility. Earthly goods: Moving to Europe, he lived in a huge wooden ashram on the Dutch-German border. At one time, he was believed to be worth about UK £2 billion

(AUD$4,949,030,184), but he openly said the money would be ploughed back into promoting TM!"⁶⁸

Give yourself permission to immediately walk away from anything that gives you bad vibes. There is no need to explain or make sense of it. Just trust that little inner voice when it talks to you.

— Anonymous

---

⁶⁸ http://www.timesonline.co.uk/section/0,,1,00.html

Drawing by Tony Talifero

CHAPTER EIGHT

The Three Christological Heresies

By way of repetition, remember, one of the most crucial questions that you can ask anybody on this planet is, "Who do you say Jesus Christ is?" Even the Lord Jesus himself asked same question! In Matthew 22:42, when he was speaking to the religious leaders of his day, he asked them, *"What do you think about the Christ? Whose Son is He?"* One needs to be able to give the correct answer, which is absolutely paramount, as the answer given may determine where one will spend Eternity!

It's good to know that the historical record of the Church provides us with a full account of how, despite a protracted period of years and at times great controversy regarding the person of Christ, clearly provides for us the correct understanding that we have today. During the long passage of time, every possible interpretation of the biblical data under discussion was examined and its elements of truth were sifted out and preserved, while the elements of error, or heresy, which perverted it were exposed and discarded by the Church.

Before one can fully and correctly understand the nature of Christ, one must first seek to understand the nature of what is called the 'Godhead'? To help I will define 'God' according to the three main views of understanding, but to do so, I will have to use some theological terms.

Firstly, there is what was called 'MODALISM'[69]. This is a false teaching that emphasises the UNITY of God, to the destruction of the true TRINITY of God. It has, over time, resulted in what has become known as UNITARIANISM[70]. It is a doctrine, or teaching, that can vary and range from a belief system which says, "Jesus was given divine powers by God" to another system that says, "Jesus was just a man like any other man, and his goodness was simply just part of his personality".

Secondly, there is what is known as 'TRINITARIANISM'. This is the doctrine, or teaching, which believes correctly in the 'Tri-unity' of God. It emphasises the sound Biblical view that God is ONE, PERSONAL and TRIUNE, that is he is 'THREE-IN-ONE" – the Father, Son and Holy Spirit.[71]

Thirdly, and along with the first, it is also a false belief and is known as 'TRITHEISM'[72]. This is the belief that there are, 'three

---

[69] 'Modalism' is the doctrine, or teaching that the persons of the Trinity represent only three modes or aspects of the divine revelation, not distinct and coexisting parts of the divine nature.

[70] Originally, all Unitarians were Christians who did not believe in the Holy Trinity of God (Father, Son, and Holy Ghost). Instead, they believed in the unity, or single aspect, of God. Although people have held Unitarian beliefs since the time of Jesus's death, religious groups did not form around these ideas until the mid-1500s in Transylvania and the 1600s in England.

[71] The Trinity is one of the defining doctrines of Christianity. All true believers will come to accept the doctrine of the Trinity because that is what the Scriptures teach.

[72] Tritheism is the teaching that the Godhead is really three separate beings forming three separate gods. This erring view is often misplaced by the cults for

equally powerful gods who form a trinity'. These three gods are envisaged as having separate powers, or spheres of influence, but they all work together. This teaching destroys the Trinity of God and the unity of God thus resulting in having THREE GODS - which is simply nothing more than plain old polytheism!

Definition of Heresy

The word 'heresy' is derived from the Greek word *'hairetikos'*, which originally meant 'choice'. The word later came to mean – 'the part, or school of a man's choice'. In the New Testament of the Bible, in the time of Christ, the term is used for the people who had formed parties (the sects, or cults of that time) known as the Sadducees and the Pharisees. These were the two main Jewish political and religious movements that were active in the time of Jesus, *"Then the high priest rose up, and all those who were with him (which is the sect of the Sadducees), and they were filled with indignation..."* (Acts 5:17); *'They knew me from the first, if they were willing to testify, that according to the strictest sect of our religion I lived a Pharisee."* (26:5)

The following is a summary regarding these two sects which comes from the Believe website[73]:

---

the doctrine of the Trinity which states that there is but one God in three persons: Father, Son, and Holy Spirit. The doctrine of the trinity is, by definition, monothestic. That is, it is a doctrine that affirms that there is only one God in all the Universe.

[73] http://www.mb-soft.com/believe

The Sadducees

The Sadducees were a prominent Jewish religious sect. Their beliefs included: acceptance only of the Law of Moses (the Torah) and a rejection of oral traditions; the denial of a bodily resurrection; the immortality of the soul; the existence of a spirit world: meaning there are no angels and no demons (See Mark 12:18; Luke 20:27; Acts 23:8). The Sadducees were a relatively small group, but they generally held the office of high priest as in the time of Christ. They denounced John the Baptist (Matthew 3:7-8) and Jesus Christ (Matthew 16:6, 11-12). They actively opposed Jesus Christ (Matthew 21:12; Mark 11:15; Luke 19:47) and the Apostolic Church (Acts 5:17, 33).

The Pharisees

The Pharisees were the other prominent sect of the Jews. They also opposed Jesus Christ and His teachings. They plotted His death (Matthew 12:14). They were denounced by Him as being 'hypocrites' (Matthew 23). Their characteristic teachings included: a belief in the oral (passed on by word of mouth – or, 'Oral Torah') as well as the written Law (Torah); the resurrection of the human body; the belief in the existence of a spirit world; the immortality of the soul; predestination; future rewards and punishments based upon works (See Matthew 9:11-14; 12:1-8; 16:1-12; 23; Luke 11:37-44; Acts 15:5; 23:6-8) for more detail.

Before the time of the writing of the New Testament, the word *heresy* had begun to take on its distinctively Christian sense, i.e., heresy was, "a line of thought, teaching or practice which has deviated from the mainstream of Christianity".

The Origin of Heresies

Historically, the first great 'bone of contention' that came up in the early church had to do with the Person of Christ. This became a great controversy that even tended to overtake the work of Christ, because who he really was would greatly interpret what He had actually done. As said, most early heresies based their beliefs on the assumption that Christ must be either divine or human, but He could not be both. Because these two natures in Christ seemed to be mutually exclusive, they either held to the one, while rejecting or diminishing the other. For that reason, all early heresies either ended up under-evaluating Christ's Divinity (that He was God manifest in the flesh), or His human nature, or both.

The origin of these early heresies must be seen in the context of the then current philosophies and religious views into which Jesus Christ was born. It was during the second and third centuries that the influence of Stoicism, which is a school of philosophy and spirituality, founded in 308 B.C. in Athens by one Zeno of Citium (Cyprus). Stoicism taught that living according to reason and nature is the primary good in life. It also taught indifference to suffering, which means that virtuous people can remain independent of society but they are obligated to help others. They can only become more enlightened by putting their virtue into practice in their actions with others and Platonic Thought which caused some to deny the full Deity of Christ. ('Platonic Idealism' is the theory that the substance of the reality which is around us is only a reflection of a higher truth)

For that reason, for the first three centuries in the Christian era, religious discussion centred almost entirely on the relationship between the Father and the Son, to the nearly complete neglect of their relationship with the Holy Spirit, the third person of the Trinity. As one theologian said, "The doctrine of the two natures united in one person is the key to understanding the Biblical Christ. The alternatives which we are to encounter face-to-face are: either, the two-natured Christ in history, or a strong delusion"[74].

However, we have to be honest and quick to state that throughout our study of the two natures of Christ, as with the study of the Trinity, we are faced with what some have called 'an impenetrable mystery'. The Trinity is one of the mysteries which the Scripture's teach and reveal, but they make absolutely no effort to explain it! For example, take the fact of the existence of God. In Genesis 1:1 the Bible simply says, "In the beginning God..." and it too makes absolutely no attempt at all to explain that statement! The Lord Jesus Christ has to be the most unique Person in all of the history of mankind. As the famous Saint Augustine once said concerning the doctrine of the Trinity, "Spend your life trying to understand it, and you will lose your mind; but deny it and you will lose your soul".

Please note what the late well-known and highly respected Christian author, Selwyn Hughes, had to say in the September-October 2006 issue of his 'Every Day with Jesus' Series for Friday, 6th September, after quoting, 'Then God said, "Let us make man in our image, in our likeness..." (Genesis 1:26), he wrote, "...the most important issue in the universe is that of relationships...it (his understanding of this) came about through reading a book

---

[74] Christology and Criticism, Dr. Benjamin B. Warfield, p309.

entitled The Everlasting God, written by the respected Anglican theologian, David Broughton Knox [75].

In a chapter describing the function of the Trinity he made the point that fundamentally God is a relational Being. That is the truth being hinted at in our text today, where we see that there is more than one divine Person in the Godhead. God is a community – a community of three Persons who relate to one another in perfect harmony. No quarrels, no arguments, no tensions. The Father loves the Son and gives Him everything (John 3:35). The Son always does that which pleases the Father (John 8:29). The [Holy] Spirit takes the things of the Son and shows them to us". (John 16:15)

Hughes continues, what was to him a profound and significant statement by Knox which changed his thinking: "We learn from the Trinity that relationship is the essence of reality…and therefore the essence of our existence". Hughes went on to say "Up until that moment I had always believed that the ultimate reality was truth. But I came to see that important though truth is, it is not the ultimate reality. Truth is propositional; relationship is personal. When you touch the heart of the universe you touch not simply an idea, a law, or even a thought. You touch a God who relates. There is warmth, not just wonder, at the heart of the Trinity – the warmth of interpersonal relationships".

The following is part of what Hughes wrote on the subject. "One of the better explanations of the Trinity is this. God, we know, is one God. But there stepped into the world one day 'someone' who also claimed to be God. He came from Nazareth

---

[75] Knox was principal of Moore Theological College in Sydney, NSW from 1959-1985 and was considered by some as the "Father of Contemporary Sydney Anglicanism".

and His name was Jesus. He forgave sins (something only God can do!), disclosed that He had existence before Abraham, and accepted worship as His right. Worship, remember, is for God alone. After Jesus was resurrected and had returned to heaven He sent back the Holy Spirit, who is also seen as God (2 Corinthians 13:14). He – the Holy Spirit – came into the disciples and brought with Him the resources of the Godhead, breaking the sin in their nature, molding them to holiness, pleading in prayer, and exalting the Saviour. Thus we see that God is not only One, but also Three in One: God above us, God among us, God within us. The Father in majesty, the Son in suffering, the Spirit in striving. This is the central mystery of our most holy faith. Together, and with all our hearts, let us adore the great triune God".

(See Appendix Six for a list of some of the Christian-based cults who reject and deny the Trinity)

CHAPTER NINE

The Division of Heresies

Historically, there has always been three main heresies, or false teachings, that keep unsettling the Church. Down through the centuries there has been a repetition of these three types of heresy, almost in every generation, with only very slight variations. It is interesting to note that many of those who are widely regarded as being cults today, are simply promoting variations of these exact same 'regurgitated' heresies! To explain, there are those who:

Deny Christ's Divinity

Briefly, in the Second Century AD there arose Ebionism. The Ebionites believed that poverty was a virtue and that Jesus was a prophet rather than the divine Word of God; then in the Fourth Century AD arose Arianism which was a belief held by one named Arius, who taught that Jesus was a 'created being'! Which is a foundational belief of firstly, the Seventh-Day Adventists (SDA) and secondly, of the Jehovah's Witnesses, the founder of which reputedly was Charles Taze Russell, who was involved with a Second Adventist group, which included his father as secretary!

However, in order for the SDA's to become fully recognised and accepted as an 'evangelical denomination', in recent years they have begun saying that they have 'changed their view' and now believe (but extremely vague when one examines what they actually say!) in the Trinity and the Deity of Christ! My readers need to know that this is simply a ruse on their part to make them to be more acceptable and amenable to the mainline denominations, among which they would dearly love to be accepted so they can convert them! In spite of what they say, my concern is that they still hold to their so-called Messenger, Ellen G. White's (their 'Spirit of Prophecy') teachings and her 'Three Angels Messages'[76]) Despite all of my detractors and their loud objections, I still believe truthfully and Scripturally that the SDA's are a cult!

Nestorianism (see footnotes and more following) was named for one Nestorius[77] the Patriarch of Constantinople. He taught that there were two separate persons in the incarnate Christ, one divine and the other human; then along came Socinianism proclaiming the beliefs of Laelius Socinus (d.1562 in Zürich) and of his nephew Faustus Socinus, who died 1604 in Poland. They both held skeptical views on reason and rejected orthodox teachings on the Trinity and on the divinity of Jesus.

Then followed Liberalism which attempted to adapt religious ideas to modern culture and ways of thinking. Following on its heels came Humanism – which included 'Christian humanism' which is defined as being, "...a philosophy advocating the self-fulfillment of man within the framework of Christian

---

[76] Go to our website : mandateministries.com.au for further information about Seventh-Day Adventism.

[77] Refers to theology of Nestorius of Antioch, who became Bishop of Constantinople in 428 A.D. He believed that Mary was mother only of the human Jesus, not the divine Logos and in the "two-nature" Christology.

principles"[78]; then came the issue of Unitarianism which rejects the doctrine of the Trinity. However, this belief ranges from a belief that Jesus was given divine powers by God, to a belief that Jesus was just a man like any other, and his goodness was just part of his personality. Today many Unitarians deny a personal God and instead they place their faith in the love and brotherhood of humankind, which is contrary to Christianity.

All the foregoing heresies promote a doctrine that denies the truth that Jesus Christ was God manifest in the flesh!

Deny Christ's Two Natures

In the 5th and 6th Century AD a Christian heresy called Monophysitism which was concerned the two Nature's of Christ. They accepted only the Divine Nature of Christ. They were condemned as heretics by the Fourth Ecumenical Council, convened at Nicaea in 451 AD; Eutychianism taught that Jesus had one nature which was neither human nor divine, but was a third nature; Monothelitism taught that Christ had only one will, even though he had two natures, that were both human and divine. These three teachings were condemned as being heresy by the Third Ecumenical Council at Constantinople.

The foregoing heresies have confused the two natures of Christ, the human and the divine, in that they are absorbed one into the other.

---

[78] Webster's Third New International Dictionary

Deny Christ's Humanity

Docetism taught that Jesus Christ was not a real man, but simply appeared so; Marcionism was the heresy that plagued the Church of the Second and Third centuries. It rejected the Old Testament of the Bible and denied the incarnation of God in Jesus as a human. The 'incarnation' is the Christian doctrine that affirms that the eternal Son of God became human in the person of Jesus of Nazareth and that the historical Christ is at once fully God and fully man; Gnosticism – there are some elements of Second Century Gnosticism which are pre-Christian. The word gnostic comes from the Greek word for knowledge 'gnosis' referring to the idea that there is special, hidden knowledge that only a select few may possess; Apollinarianism taught that Christ was a human soul but had a divine mind. Espoused by Apollinarius (c.310-390 AD); Monarchianism was a Second Century belief which was taught by some in early Christianity and it centres around God as being one person and that God is the single and only ruler; Patripassianism is the belief that God the Father and Son are simply different aspects of God. The implication of this is contrary to Scripture and implies that God the Father suffered on the cross! Sabellianism, after one named Sabellius, who taught widely in the Third Century that God is one being, one person, who successively takes on three different forms or manifestations; Adoptions is another belief, from the Second and Third Centuries AD, teaching that Jesus was born the same as any other human, and is not therefore a deity, or God manifest, or come, in the flesh. It teaches that God later gave Jesus supernatural powers at his water baptism when God chose him to become his 'adopted' son; Dynamic Monarchianism teaches that God is the Father and that Jesus is only a man, and it denies the personal subsistence of the

Logos (Greek: *logos* means 'word') which is a symbol for Christ, 'the word incarnate', or the 'word made Flesh'. They also taught that the Holy Spirit was a 'force' or 'the presence' of God the Father. Present day groups who fall generally into this category are the Jehovah's Witnesses, Christadelphians, and the Unitarians.

All the foregoing names were usually coined from the name of the individuals who promoted and led the type of heresy listed and have since been applied to them by the church in general. Space does not permit a large amount of detail relating to each school of thought. However, it is suffice to say, that all of these heresies ended up 'dividing' the 'theanthropic God-Man (the word theanthropic is a theological term meaning, 'the God-Man') who is none other than the true Lord Jesus Christ!

The Christological Zig-Zag

Renowned Biblical scholar and theologian, Dr. Benjamin B. Warfield, summarized the rising and falling of these various early heresies as follows: "To the onlooker from this distance of time, the main line of progress of the debate takes on an odd appearance of what can be described as a steady zig-zag advance. Arising out of the embers of the Arian controversy, there is first vigorously asserted, over against the reduction of our Lord to the dimensions of a creature, the pure Deity of His spiritual nature (Apollinarianism – more to come). By this there is at once provoked, in the interests of the integrity of our Lord's humanity, the equally vigorous assertion of the completeness of His human nature as the bearer of His Deity (Nestorianism – also more to come). This in turn provokes, in the interest of the oneness of His person, an equally vigorous assertion of the conjunction of these two natures in a single individual (which led to what is called Eutychianism[79]); from all of which there gradually emerges at last, by a series of corrections, the balanced statement of Chalcedon (which was the 4th Ecumenical Council in 451 AD which defined the two natures [human and divine] of Christ), recognizing at once in its "without confusion, without Deity conversion, eternally and inseparably" the union in the person of Christ of a complete Deity and a complete humanity constituting a single person without prejudice to the continued integrity of either nature.

The pendulum of thought had swung back and forth in ever-decreasing arcs until at last it found rest along the line of action of the fundamental force. Out of the continuous controversy of a century, there issued a balanced statement in which all the elements of the biblical representation were taken up and combined. Work so done is done for all time; and it is capable of ever-repeated demonstration that in the developed doctrine of the Two Natures and in it alone, all the biblical data are brought together in a harmonious statement in which each receives full recognition, and out of which each may derive its sympathetic exposition. This key unlocks the treasures of the biblical instruction on the person of Christ as none other can, and enables the reader as he currently scans the sacred pages to take up their declarations as they meet him, one after the other, into an

---

[79] Eutychianism refers to a set of Christian theological doctrines derived from the ideas of Eutyches of Constantinople (c. 380–456). It is his understanding of how the human and divine relate within the person of Jesus Christ. Eutyches taught that the human nature of Christ was overcome by the divine, or that Christ had a human nature but it was unlike the rest of humanity.

intelligently consistent conception of his Lord". (Christology and Criticism, p264; Parenthesis added).

The "Christological zig-zag" referred to by Warfield could be likened to the following diagram:

Condemning the Heretics and their Heresies

Heretics, or those who promote un-Biblical teachings, have been promoting their false doctrines since the church first began. As one reads through the Letters to the various churches in the New Testament, it soon becomes obvious that the authors mainly penned their letters to expose and correct wrong teachings, or false doctrines/heresies, which had deceptively and insidiously crept into the church.

Down through the centuries of the life of the church there have been many great church councils, or conferences and synods, which were convened by very learned and eminent church leaders. These were attended by leaders of the church universal, who came to openly discuss and investigate in depth, teachings that had become controversial, like those referred to in this chapter, on matters of doctrine which had entered the church and were causing great deal of confusion and division.

What most people fail to understand is that in every instance, the benchmark for these councils was set by the teachings of the leaders of the Early Church. These, of course, were the teachings in the writings of the Apostles Paul, Peter, John and Jesus' brother James and others like Mark and Luke.

When the controversial matters in question were raised in general session at such councils, and were subsequently found by the majority present to contradict the teachings of the early church leaders, then two actions by the council always resulted.

Dr Kenneth L. Gentry, Jr in his, 'The Usefulness of Creeds', says, "...creeds serve as tools of Christian education. It should be obvious that the sheer volume of the Bible (1189 chapters with over 773,000 words) forbids its full comprehension in a moment and by every Christian—or even by one supremely gifted believer in an entire lifetime. Nevertheless, the Church is commanded in the Old Testament (Shema) Deut. 6:4-25) and the New Testament Great Commission (Matt. 28:19-20) to teach the Bible's truth to others. This teaching process will necessarily deal with fundamental, selected truths at first, truths such as are outlines and organized in a creed".

Firstly, at the historical Councils a 'position paper' was drawn up and issued stating the final decision of the council. These 'position papers' immediately became the Creeds of the Church of that time and are still used by the church down to this day. Secondly, the perpetrators, or initiators of what was proven by the councils to be heresy, were asked publicly to recant their heresy. By refusing to do so, many of the perpetrators of what had been declared as heresy, were stripped of their office in the church, with some even being excommunicated (which means to be put out of the church). The following highlights the Creeds of some of the councils:

Council of Nicaea AD 324

The Council was convened by the Roman Emperor Constantine. He called the Council to consider and if it was possible, to settle the Arian controversy (heresy) that was causing division in the church, teaching that 'Jesus Christ was a created being'. The council resolved and gave the church the first great Ecumenical Creed[80] which states:

"We believe in one God the Father Almighty, Maker of heaven and earth, and of all things visible and invisible. And in one Lord Jesus Christ, the only-begotten Son of God, begotten of the Father before all worlds, God of God, Light of Light, Very God of Very God, begotten, not made, being of one substance with the Father by whom all things were made; who for us men, and for our salvation, came down from heaven, and was incarnate by the Holy Spirit of the Virgin Mary, and was made man, and was crucified also for us under Pontius Pilate. He suffered and was buried, and the third day he rose again according to the Scriptures, and ascended into heaven, and sitteth on the right hand of the Father. And he shall come again with glory to judge both the quick and the dead, whose kingdom shall have no end. And we believe in the Holy Spirit, the Lord and Giver of Life, who proceedeth from the Father and the Son, who with the Father and the Son together is worshipped and glorified, who spoke by the prophets. And we believe one holy catholic and apostolic Church. We acknowledge one baptism for the remission of sins. And we look for the resurrection of the dead, and the life of the world to come. Amen".

---

[80] The three major ones that still referred to in most mainline denominations today are: The Apostle's Creed, The Nicene Creed and the Athanasian Creed.

First Council of Constantinople AD 381

This Council was convened by Emperor Theodosius the Great, to correct the errors of Apollinarianism and Macedonianism.[81] At the close of this council, Emperor Theodosius issued an imperial decree declaring that the churches should be restored to those bishops who confessed the equal Divinity of the Father, the Son, and the Holy Spirit, and who held communion with Nectarius of Constantinople and other important church leaders whom he named.

---

[81] Macedonianism: A 4th-century Christian heresy that denied the full personality and divinity of the Holy Spirit. According to this heresy, the Holy Spirit was created by the Son and was thus subordinate to the Father and the Son. In Orthodox Christian theology, God is one in essence but three in Person—Father, Son, and Holy Spirit, who are distinct and equal. (the online Encyclopaedia Brittanica)

Council of Ephesus AD 431

This Council was presided over by Cyril, the Bishop of Alexandria, and was called to deal with Nestorianism which over emphasised the human nature of Jesus at the expense of the divine. The Council denounced Nestorius' teaching as erroneous as he taught that Mary gave birth to a man, Jesus Christ, and not God the 'Logos' ('The Word', the Son of God). The Logos they said, only dwelt in Christ, as in a Temple (this meant for them that Christ, was only Theophoros: or, the "Bearer of God".) Consequently, this would mean that Mary should be called "Christotokos" meaning the mother of Christ and not "Theotokos" the "Mother of God" as she is.

The Council decreed that Jesus was one person, not two separate 'people': complete God and complete man, with a rational soul and body. That Mary is "Theotokos" because she gave birth not to man, but to God as a man. The union of the two natures of Christ took place in such a fashion that one does not disturb the other. The Council also declared the text of the Nicene Creed, decreed at both the First and Second Ecumenical Councils, to be complete and forbade any additional change (i.e., there were to be no additions or deletions) to it. In addition, it condemned the teaching of one named Pelagius, whose teachings are now known as Pelagianism. His was the belief that original sin did not taint human nature and that a mortal is still capable of choosing good or evil without special Divine aid.

Council of Chalcedon AD 451

This Council was convened by Emperor Marcian, with the reluctant approval of Leo of Rome, who sent three bishops and two presbyters appointed to be his representatives. The Council condemned Eutychianism, and gave the church another creedal statement on Christology which has stood the test of time. The Chalcedonian statement has largely become the orthodox creed of Protestantism, which states:

"Therefore, following the holy fathers, we all with one accord teach men to acknowledge one and the same Son, our Lord Jesus Christ, at once complete in Godhead and complete in manhood, truly God and truly man, consisting also of a reasonable soul and body; of one substance with the Father as regards his Godhead, and at the same time of one substance with us as regards his manhood; like us in all respects, apart from sin; as regards his Godhead, begotten of the Father before the ages, but yet as regards his manhood begotten, for us men and for our salvation, of Mary the Virgin, the God-bearer; one and the same Christ, Son, Lord, Only-begotten, recognized in two natures, without confusion, without change, without division, without separation; the distinction of natures being in no way annulled by the union, but rather the characteristics of each nature being preserved and coming together to form one person and subsistence, not as parted or separated into two persons, but one and the same Son and Only-begotten God the Word, Lord Jesus Christ; even as the prophets from earliest times spoke of him, and our Lord Jesus Christ himself taught us, and the creed of the fathers has handed down to us".

Second Council of Constantinople AD 680

The Council was called by the Emperor Constantine Pogonatus, and was directed against Monothelitism. The Tenth of Fourteen Statements issued by the Council reads: *"If anyone does not confess his belief that our lord Jesus Christ, who was crucified in his human flesh, is truly God and the Lord of glory and one of the members of the holy Trinity: let him be anathema"* ('anathema' is a Greek word and means: to be formally set apart; banished, exiled, excommunicated or denounced). It is very often misinterpreted to mean accursed. The correct and broader meaning of the term is applied to a person who has been 'set apart, banished and considered beyond the judgment and help of the community'.

The Frankford Synod (AD 794)

This Synod is also known as the 'Council of Dort' after the name of the town in which it was convened in Holland. It was convened by Charlemagne or, Charles the Great, a Carolingian (Franks) monarch [742-814 AD] who established a substantial empire in both France and Germany. He was to be eventually crowned as Emperor of the Holy Roman Empire. The Council condemned the heresy of 'Adoptions'.

'Adoptions' is the heretical, or wrong belief, that Jesus was born just as any other human, and is not a deity, or God, and that God later gave him supernatural powers at his water baptism in the river Jordan by John the Baptist, when God then chose Jesus to become his adopted son!

In conclusion, one can readily see that by comparing ancient and contemporary heresies, just how Satan the devil has constantly tried to hide and corrupt the true theanthropic nature of Christ, in that he was both divine and human, because, if either nature could be 'corrupted', then it would mean that true Salvation has been totally destroyed!

"We are not permitted to cherish any doctrine after our own will, nor to choose that which another person has introduced from their own private fancy. In the Lord's apostles we possess our authority. Even they did not choose to introduce anything from themselves, but faithfully delivered to the nations the discipline which they had received from Christ. If, therefore, even an angel from heaven should preach any other gospel, he would be called accursed by us." - Tertullian, c. A.D. 200

CHAPTER TEN

The Biblical Christ

All Christians, who are truly Born-again of the Spirit of God, accept without question the Lord Jesus Christ's Godhood, or Deity. Deity is a term which indicates that Christ's nature is divine from all eternity, although he took on human nature at his incarnation - whilst still retaining his deity (John 1:1,14,18)[82].

The Scriptural basis for this belief is clearly defined by the Apostle John in his Chapter 1:1, where he records, *"In the beginning was the Word, and the Word was with God, and the Word was God"*. Cults who deny the Divinity of Christ, like the Jehovah's Witnesses, who have changed this verse in their own discredited re-write of the Bible, called the 'New World Translation' to read, "In [the] beginning the Word was, and the Word was with God, and the Word was a God"[83]. Therefore, to have a different 'Jesus' to the one in the Bible, is not to have Jesus at all!

In fact, the literal translation of the Greek to English, reads, *"In beginning was the Word, and the Word was toward the God, and god was the Word"* note "God was the Word"! To render this verse as the Jehovah's Witnesses have done, is deceptive and dishonest, for

---

[82] See Appendix Two for a chart clearly showing that 'Jesus is Yahweh'

as the reader can see, the original Greek language simply does not say "a God" as they do! (Text in Italics quoted verbatim from what is regarded as the reliable Westcott and Hort translation published by Jehovah's Witnesses in their own book, "The Kingdom Interlinear Translation of the Greek Scriptures", Watchtower Bible and Tract Society of New York, Inc., First Edition, 1969)

All true Christians accept the fact that Jesus came as a man to dwell on earth for a time. This belief is well justified in the words of John 1:14, *"And the Word became flesh and dwelt among us..."* Therefore, Jesus Christ was not just "a god" (as if there were any other gods!) because He is God truly manifest in the flesh! As God, Jesus Christ was complete Deity, fully God, and therefore He has to have a Divine Nature. One should always remember, with repetition for emphasis, that Jesus Christ is known in theological terms as being *Theanthropic*, which means that Christ was both human and divine in nature. He embodied deity in human form. Again, the word *Theanthropic* derives from two Greek words: *theos* meaning 'god', and *anthropos* meaning 'man', thus we have in Jesus Christ the 'God-Man'.

Therefore, as a man, Jesus Christ, whilst dwelling here on earth, was complete humanity. He was fully man, with a human nature (but not the fallen sinful human nature or 'flesh' mentioned in Romans Chapter 7). Therefore, He is the God Man as He was TWO natures in ONE person. This fact the Christian accepts by faith from the very Word of God, all the time knowing full well, that a clearly logical description offered for such a belief will, for many without true faith working in their lives, will be at best perhaps somewhat obscure.

F.F. Bruce (Frederick Fyvie Bruce, 1910-1990) a respected Bible scholar and Christian apologist (Elected a Fellow of the

British Academy, where he served as President of the Society for Old Testament Study, and also as President of the Society for New Testament Study) is absolutely correct when he says: "Our conception of God must fall far short of His real being, and our language about Him must fall short of our conception". The prophet Isaiah in 40:18 says, *"To whom then will you liken God, or what likeness compare with Him?"* Even so, the language of the creeds is still to be commended for their descriptions of Jesus, the 'God Man'. Inadequate is the language of the various heretics and their teachings.

Therefore, in the ancient creedal statements of Christ, it is safe to say that the Scripture representations of Christ as MAN finds harmonious adjustment and acceptance. It is also important to realize that these creedal statements were never meant to be additions to the Biblical record, but to be amplifications of it.

Long before the Council of Chalcedon, Christians lived in the faith that Christ was, and must be, essentially related to both God and man. Therefore, contrary to what the deceived members of the various cults say, Chalcedon never departed from the Gospel, nor did it add to it. What was stated technically at Chalcedon in 451 AD was known implicitly by the church at Corinth as far back as 51 AD. Someone has said, "No doubt we can say more about Christ than what Chalcedon says to-day, but we dare not say any less"!

The orthodox (the traditional or accepted beliefs) doctrine, of the person of Christ, has been the common heritage of the church since the Council of Chalcedon in 451 AD. As we have seen by the fact of its many heretical opponents; it is not a doctrine which was arrived at easily, but one which required very long, intense and patient study of the Scriptures. This was then followed by lengthy and lively debate in the church councils. History records that numerous other solutions were tried and found wanting. The same with the 'false christs' of today's contemporary cults. They are also found wanting when it comes to their understanding of what constitutes true Salvation!

The writer believes that there is much truth in the comment made by the eminent Dr. A.P. Peabody (graduated Harvard University in 1826, then studied three years in the divinity school... was in time appointed preacher to the university and professor of Christian Morals. He received his degree of Doctorate of Divinity (D.D.) from Harvard in 1852, and his Doctorate of Laws and Letters (LL.D.) from the University of Rochester in 1863) concerning these many Christological heresies, when he said, "The canon of infidelity was closed almost as soon as that of the Scriptures. Modern unbelievers have done little more than repeat the long-exploded heresies of former centuries"!

After an exhaustive examination of the early Christological heresies, well-known and respected Christian author Dr. Loraine Boettner concluded: "The foregoing survey of the erroneous views concerning the Person of Christ would seem to show that history has exhausted the possibilities of heresy and that future denials of the doctrine must be, in essence, only variations of views which have already been advanced and refuted"[84]. So, when wise King Solomon said, "There is nothing new under the sun" he was absolutely right!

We as Christians, perhaps need to make an effort to understand something of these repetitive heresies and what constituted their fatal errors. We need to think them through,

---

[84] Studies in Theology, p265

along with what our early church fathers taught, because until our Lord returns, heresies are simply going to keep 'popping up' (so to speak) and re-appearing in one form or another in every generation with subtle differences! This view is supported by F.F. Bruce when he said, "The various heresies that sprang up in the earliest Christian centuries are by no means out of date. They reappear regularly in one form or another from generation to generation" (The Spreading Flame, p314).

We conclude this part of our discussion with the exhortation of Bible author Jude, who wrote, *"Beloved, while I was very diligent to write to you concerning our common salvation, I found it necessary to write to you exhorting you to contend earnestly for the faith which was once for all delivered to the saints. For certain men have crept in unnoticed, who long ago were marked out for this condemnation, ungodly men, who turn the grace of our God into lewdness and deny the only Lord God and our Lord Jesus Christ."* (3-4)

Let me ask a question: Who in their right mind, would want to die for a 'false christ' or a 'false prophet'? Sadly, many down through the centuries have done just that and are still doing so today! Knowing the True Biblical Jesus was so important to the members of the early Church that they were prepared to stand and die for him, as the following account reveals:!

The Bold Martyrdom of Polycarp of Smyrna

Polycarp was 86 years of age when he stood before a Roman proconsul condemned to die. The proconsul felt sorry for him. He gave him repeated instructions on how to avoid the punishment that was in store for him. Polycarp was unimpressed. "Since you keep wasting your time urging me on and pretend not to know who and what I am, listen to me announce with boldness: "I am a Christian. But if you want to learn what the doctrines of Christianity are, appoint me a day, and you shall hear them." This irritated the proconsul. He decided to put a little pressure on the old man. "I have wild beasts at hand. I will throw you to them if you don't repent." No effect. "Call them, then. We're not used to repenting of what is good in order to adopt what is evil."

That was enough for the proconsul. No more Mr. Nice Guy! "If you won't repent, I'll have you burned with fire, since you have no regard for the wild beasts!" No better. The 86-year-old Polycarp was up to a face-to-face confrontation, "You threaten me with fire that burns for an hour, then goes out after a little while. You're ignorant, however, of the fire of the coming judgment and of eternal punishment, reserved for the ungodly. What are you waiting for? Bring out whatever you want."

When he spoke these things, and many others like them, he was filled with confidence and joy. His face was so full of grace that not only did it seem like he wasn't troubled by anything said to him, but the proconsul was astonished. The proconsul really couldn't take any more, and he turned Polycarp over to the stadium crowd, which Polycarp had insulted minutes earlier. He had called the people atheists and told the proconsul that they weren't worthy to hear the doctrines of Christianity. The crowd, in a fevered rage, brought enough wood to build a bonfire, and Polycarp was burned alive at the stake.

CHAPTER ELEVEN

When Confronted by the Cultist

When you are approached or confronted, as most people will be at some time during their life or Christian walk and your faith is challenged by a member of a cult group, remember that his only purpose in speaking to you is to 'convert' you to his way of thinking and try to get you to become a member of his group or cult! The manner in which we conduct ourselves in such an encounter should be as outlined for us in 1st Peter 3:13-15:

"Now who is there to harm you if you are zealous for what is right? But even if you suffer for righteousness' sake, you will be blessed. Have no fear of them, nor be troubled, but in your hearts reverence Christ as Lord. Always be prepared to make a defence to anyone who calls you to ac-count for the hope that is in you, yet do it with gentleness and reverence".

Therefore, we should endeavour to try to make the foregoing counsel our basis for communicating the True Gospel to others, for our Gospel teaches us that:

- We are not to fear anyone
- We should set ourselves apart for witness and the service of the Lord Jesus Christ

- We should provide an answer to everyone who queries the hope we have within.
- Remember, if we can't give an immediate answer on some point, we should simply admit that we don't know the answer and that we will obtain one and come back to them with it. Then we should do just that!
- We must show gentleness and reverence to all people
- We must recognize that there will be times when we must confidently take a bold stand for the true Faith!

The Scriptures clearly record for us that in the New Testament the church was being bombarded from all directions by pagan religion and overzealous Jewish leaders. Not the least of them was one young man, Saul of Tarsus, who was to go on to become the great Apostle Paul after he encountered the true Messiah, the real Lord Jesus! The church in those days dealt with cultic theology in the aforementioned manner and from the writer's personal experience, this counsel is still valid for today's confrontations with heresy.

Notice how three Christians, Peter, John and Philip, acted when they were confronted by paganism in Acts Chapter 8. Especially take note of the way in which Peter and Philip conducted themselves. Then, in Chapter 9 the incidents at Lydda and Joppa, and again more boldly in Chapter 13:4-12 which records Paul's admonishment: *"So, being sent out by the Holy Spirit, they went down to Seleucia, and from there they sailed to Cyprus. And when they arrived in Salamis, they preached the word of God in the synagogues of the Jews. They also had John as their assistant. Now when they had gone through the island to Paphos, they found a certain sorcerer, a false prophet, a Jew whose name was Bar-Jesus, who was with the proconsul, Sergius Paulus, an intelligent man. This man called for*

Barnabas and Saul and sought to hear the word of God. But Elymas the sorcerer (for so his name is translated) withstood them, seeking to turn the proconsul away from the faith. Then Saul, who also is called Paul, filled with the Holy Spirit, looked intently at him and said, "O full of all deceit and all fraud, you son of the devil, you enemy of all righteousness, will you not cease perverting the straight ways of the Lord? And now, indeed, the hand of the Lord is upon you, and you shall be blind, not seeing the sun for a time." And immediately a dark mist fell on him, and he went around seeking someone to lead him by the hand. Then the proconsul believed, when he saw what had been done, being astonished at the teaching of the Lord."

A further example is recorded for us in Acts 14:8-18, *"And in Lystra a certain man without strength in his feet was sitting, a cripple from his mother's womb, who had never walked. This man heard Paul speaking. Paul, observing him intently and seeing that he had faith to be healed, said with a loud voice, "Stand up straight on your feet!" And he leaped and walked. Now when the people saw what Paul had done, they raised their voices, saying in the Lycaonian language, "The gods have come down to us in the likeness of men!" And Barnabas they called Zeus, and Paul, Hermes, because he was the chief speaker. Then the priest of Zeus, whose temple was in front of their city, brought oxen and garlands to the gates, intending to sacrifice with the multitudes. But when the apostles Barnabas and Paul heard this, they tore their clothes and ran in among the multitude, crying out and saying, "Men, why are you doing these things? We also are men with the same nature as you, and preach to you that you should turn from these useless things to the living God, who made the heaven, the earth, the sea, and all things that are in them, who in bygone generations allowed all nations to walk in their own ways. Nevertheless He did not leave Himself without witness, in that He did good, gave us rain from heaven and fruitful seasons, filling our hearts with food and gladness." And with these sayings they could scarcely restrain the multitudes from sacrificing to them".*

The reader will find other examples recorded in the Book of Acts which show just how the early Saints conducted themselves when their theology, or belief system, was being confronted, opposed and threatened. See Acts 15:5; Chapters 19, 20, and 21:18-26.

CHAPTER TWELVE

How Then Should We Deal With Them?

The writer believes, as in all matters of spiritual warfare, that we must be prepared and know the enemy and his tactics. Good preparation will always cost you something - in this case, you have to make the effort and it will cost you your time and you're your money! For yourself and for the sake of your family, your friends and others, you must know something of what the various cults believe and have some knowledge of their false teachings.

For starters one should become acquainted with the facts about the group that the cultist who is confronting you is from? You have to do this if you want to be successful in saving, perhaps not only your own physical and spiritual life, but the lives of others too. If you are already a Born-again Christian, then you need to make every effort to know well your own Christian faith. A good Christian is one who knows not only what he believes, but why he believes it! This will enable you to take on board most of the information that has been given to this point and gives you an advantage in setting your loved one, or friend, free from cultic bondage. However, if you have not yet accepted Jesus Christ as your Lord and Saviour, you have probably realized already that you have a quite a job ahead of you. That's why I recommend that if you are dealing with a cult that claims to be 'Christian' you should think about making a quality decision to become capable of winning spiritual battles, not only in your cult member's life, but in your own life and that of your family! This is why, at the risk of seeming to be repetitious, I have included in this revision of the book, the chapter, 'How to Become a True Christian' just for you.

Perhaps you may consider pausing in your reading here and turning to that chapter and finding for yourself the way for you to get to know the one who said, "I am the way and the truth and the Life. No one comes to the Father except through me."! The speaker, or course, was the Lord Jesus![85]

If you are a Christian, or not, in order for you to be effective in your witness to any member of a cult, you will need to know something of the cult, or group's background:
(a)   Their beginning
(b)   Their leader/s and his/their background
(c)   Their habit of 'twisting' Christian terminology
(d)   Their learned 'interpretation process' of Scripture, which is common to all the cults who use the Bible - unless they have their own, usually spurious, translation that has been changed in order to support their own teachings.
(e)   Their pat answers, which they have learned by wrote and are parroting, so you can show them why their beliefs are wrong.

One should make an effort beforehand to find out from others the most effective way in which to lead a particular cultist to know the truth and to be set free! Remember that all cultists will use

---

[85] John 14:6

terminology with which you, if you are a Christian, will find familiar. It would help you to understand what they have completely redefined with their terminology. It would be much more difficult for the non-Christian to understand where they are coming from!

What they have been taught will be the key points, although wrong, that fits the system of belief which they have embraced. Please remember that when you are speaking with a cultist, that he will be constantly mentally re-interpreting the Christian terminology that you may use. He will be 'mentally translating' what you are saying into the meanings he has been taught by his particular cult group.

For example, when speaking with a member of the Moonies cult, you may quote the instance when the Lord Jesus said to Nicodemus, *"You must be born again..."* (John 3). A true Christian understands and knows exactly what the term *Born again* means and what had to be done for one to be spiritually *Born again*. He knows that he had to pray to God and repent and ask forgiveness for his personal sins, or shortcomings, and ask the Lord Jesus Christ to come into his heart to be both his Lord and Saviour[86]. However, for the Moonie, the expression 'Born-again' only means that he mentally accepts that he was 'born-again' from the very first moment that he began to read Sun Myung Moon's book, the 'Divine Principle'!

Another classic example. Almost everyone of Jehovah's Witnesses (JW) today, do not believe that they can be Born-again! According to their belief system, there were only ever a limited

---

[86] See 'How to Become a True Christian' in Chapter 18, p201

number who had the chance of being 'Born-again' and had received a 'Heavenly Hope'. They had this mind-set, because they were taught, un-Biblically and therefore heretically, that up until the early 1930's, that there would only ever be 144,000 of them in the world in total (see Revelation 7:4)! This is one of their foundational teachings. However, by 1934 the JW leaders knew that at their then growth rate, they would soon exceed that number and they had to do something about it!

So, their Governing Body, at the 1935 Convention in Washington, D.C., announced they had "new light from God" and that there would now be 'two classes' of JW! All those who were members until 1935 would from that time onward be known as the, 'Heavenly Class' (or the 'Anointed Class'). The JW's falsely believe that the 144,000 are the only ones who go to Heaven!

Today, the JW will tell you that all who became JW's after the 1935 date, make up what they refer to as being an 'Earthly Class' of people, whom they refer to as 'The Great Crowd'. Such people do not expect, nor do they have a hope of ever going to Heaven. Their belief is that they are to remain here on earth and be tasked with restoring it to the same 'paradise condition' which existed in the Garden of Eden during Adam and Eve's time. This, they believe, will occur immediately after the 'soon' coming Battle of Armageddon which will destroy 'this worldly system of things'!

For the JW's there is but one exception about being 'Born-again' – but not by the Spirit of God in the true sense! They have been taught that one can only be classified as being 'Born-again' today if he has been 'chosen' to join the 'Heavenly Flock'! Their teaching is that this can only be achieved if one of those still alive from the pre-1935 era, who 'belong' to the 'Heavenly Flock' (they would have to be now more than 90 years-of-age) 'loses his place' by committing serious sin! This is because they have been taught that to be one of the 144,000 one would have to have attained to 'an age of understanding' which they said initially (when I was involved with them), would have to be around 14 years-old to qualify! The age was 'pegged' as being a person 12-14 years-old!

The JW reasoning behind this was that if one of the so-called 'Heavenly Class' were to commit a sin like adultery, murder, or something similar. If they did, their law required them to be disfellowshipped, or excommunicated, from the organisation and would disqualify them from going to Heaven when they died!

The JW's believe that the act of disfellowshipping[87] a person of the 'Heavenly Class' would create a 'vacancy' which would have to be 'filled'! Of this, they say, it would be 'someone' who is a JW and "in good standing" who would be 'observed to be of the anointed' (by who?) and therefore they would take the disfellowshipped person's place in the 144,000! I often would wonder how they kept count and how they would choose someone to be the substitute? I think it's all very strange don't you?

Remember, when in discussion with a cultist that communication is not what you actually say, but what they think you are saying and or course *vice versa*! It's been said that words are just linguistic symbols and to give words meaning it depends on the context in which they are used. So don't just merely listen to the words that people use and assume that just because their terminology seems similar to your own, that it means what you understand it to mean. People caught up in the cults invariably

---

[87] The Jehovah's Witness term for 'Excommunication'

understand something vastly different from what you understand and because of it, are probably well on their way, sadly and unfortunately, to an everlasting separation from God, which means to spend Eternity in Hell!

Many people think that when they die - as we all will one day, that they are automatically going to go to Heaven to be with God! How often have you heard people who are obviously not Christians, say things like, "I know he's up there with the Man Upstairs" or, "She's in a better place now and watching over me"!

Then there are others who think merely because they have lived a good life, occasionally gone to church and are perhaps familiar with some of the language and stories from the Bible who will say things like, "I hope I've done enough to make it to Heaven when I die?" and "I know I'll get to see my Mum and Dad again?" Sadly, nothing could be further from the truth, unless you are Born-again, you will perish for all Eternity![88]

It is therefore, <u>imperative</u> for one to know God's Word and what it clearly and simply teaches about who go to Heaven and why? To gain such knowledge and for it to be effective and fruitful, one must be able to teach it clearly as truth. Please read again, the already quoted Scripture from Acts 14:8 15 & 18 and then take note of Chapter 17:16-20, 32-33 which says:

"Now while Paul waited for them at Athens, his spirit was provoked within him when he saw that the city was given over to idols. Therefore he reasoned in the synagogue with the Jews and with the Gentile worshipers, and in the marketplace daily with those who happened to be there. Then certain Epicurean and Stoic philosophers encountered him.

---

[88] John 3:1-8

And some said, "What does this babbler want to say?" Others said, "He seems to be a proclaimer of foreign gods," because he preached to them Jesus and the resurrection. And they took him and brought him to the Areopagus, saying, "May we know what this new doctrine is of which you speak? For you are bringing some strange things to our ears. Therefore we want to know what these things mean." For all the Athenians and the foreigners who were there spent their time in nothing else but either to tell or to hear some new thing ... And when they heard of the resurrection of the dead, some mocked, while others said, "We will hear you again on this matter." So Paul departed from among them. However, some men joined him and believed, among them Dionysius the Areopagite, a woman named Damaris, and others with them".

Therefore, in summary, to effectively communicate the true Gospel to a cultist, or anyone else, we have to:

(a) Understand something of the individual cult you are dealing with.

(b) Understand something of the problem of discernment so that we can point out the differences.

(c) Be competent to clearly communicate the truth of the Gospel.

To know and interpret the Bible correctly is paramount if one is to be able to clearly and confidently set forth what the Bible teaches. We must be able to demonstrate the truth of Christianity, as Paul counsels in 2nd Timothy 3:16-17, *"All Scripture is given by inspiration of God, and is profit-able for doctrine, for reproof, for correction, for instruction in righteousness, that the man (or woman) of God may be complete, thoroughly equipped for every good work"*

(Parenthesis added).

The early church folk not only knew how to interpret the Word of God, but how to teach it as absolute truth. Why was that so? Simply because they were all Born-again! Note what it says in Acts 8:25-39:

'So when they had testified and preached the word of the Lord, they returned to Jerusalem, preaching the gospel in many villages of the Samaritans. Now an angel of the Lord spoke to Philip, saying, "Arise and go toward the south along the road which goes down from Jerusalem to Gaza." This is desert. So he arose and went. And behold, a man of Ethiopia, a eunuch of great authority under Candace the queen of the Ethiopians, who had charge of all her treasury, and had come to Jerusalem to worship, was returning. And sitting in his chariot, he was reading Isaiah the prophet. Then the Spirit said to Philip, "Go near and overtake this chariot." So Philip ran to him, and heard him reading the prophet Isaiah, and said, "Do you understand what you are reading?" And he said, "How can I, unless someone guides me?" And he asked Philip to come up and sit with him. The place in the Scripture which he read was this: "He was led as a sheep to the slaughter; And as a lamb before its shearer is silent, So He opened not His mouth. In His humiliation His justice was taken away, And who will declare His generation? For His life is taken from the earth." So the eunuch answered Philip and said, "I ask you, of whom does the prophet say this, of himself or of some other man?"

Then Philip opened his mouth, and beginning at this Scripture, preached Jesus to him. Now as they went down the road, they came to some water. And the eunuch said, "See, here is water. What hinders me from being baptized?" Then Philip said, "If you believe with all your heart, you may." And he answered and said, "I believe that Jesus Christ is the Son of God." So he commanded the chariot to stand still. And both Philip and the eunuch went down into the water, and he baptized him. Now when they came up out of the water, the Spirit of the Lord caught

Philip away, so that the eunuch saw him no more; and he went on his way rejoicing".

The reason he was able to go on his way rejoicing was simply because he was Born-again! Another fine example as to how we should approach the Word of God is found in Acts 17:10-12 which says:

"Then the brethren immediately sent Paul and Silas away by night to Berea. When they arrived, they went into the synagogue of the Jews. These were more fair-minded than those in Thessalonica, in that they received the word with all readiness, and searched the Scriptures daily to find out whether these things were so. Therefore many of them believed, and also not a few of the Greeks, prominent women as well as men".

Another is found in Acts 18:24-26: *"Now a certain Jew named Apollos, born at Alexandria, an eloquent man and mighty in the Scriptures, came to Ephesus. This man had been instructed in the way of the Lord; and being fervent in spirit, he spoke and taught accurately the things of the Lord, though he knew only the baptism of John. So he began to speak boldly in the synagogue. When Aquila and Priscilla heard him, they took him aside and explained to him the way of God more accurately".*

To have a sound working knowledge of basic Christian doctrines, or teachings, is the only proven and effective antidote to counter the false teachings of the cults. To illustrate the point, please note what Paul wrote to Timothy in 1st Timothy 4:1-16:

"Now the Spirit expressly says that in latter times some will depart from the faith, giving heed to deceiving spirits and doctrines of demons, speaking lies in hypocrisy, having their own conscience seared with a hot iron, forbidding to marry, and commanding to abstain from foods which God created to be received with thanks-giving by those who believe and know the truth. For every creature of God is good, and nothing is to be refused if it is received with thanksgiving; for it is sanctified by the word

of God and prayer. If you instruct the brethren in these things, you will be a good minister of Jesus Christ, nourished in the words of faith and of the good doctrine which you have carefully followed. But reject profane and old wives' fables, and exercise yourself toward godliness. For bodily exercise profits a little, but godliness is profitable for all things, having promise of the life that now is and of that which is to come. This is a faithful saying and worthy of all acceptance. For to this end we both labor and suffer reproach, because we trust in the living God, who is the Savior of all men, especially of those who believe. These things command and teach. Let no one despise your youth, but be an example to the believers in word, in conduct, in love, in spirit, in faith, in purity. Till I come, give attention to reading, to exhortation, to doctrine ... Meditate on these things; give yourself entirely to them, that your progress may be evident to all. Take heed to your-self and to the doctrine. Continue in them, for in doing this you will save both yourself and those who hear you".

Note also what it says of the times we live in today in 2nd Timothy 3:1-17:

"*But know this, that in the last days perilous times will come: For men will be lovers of themselves, lovers of money, boasters, proud, blasphemers, disobedient to parents, unthankful, unholy, unloving, unforgiving, slanderers, without self-control, brutal, despisers of good, traitors, headstrong, haughty, lovers of pleasure rather than lovers of God, having a form of godliness but denying its power. And from such people turn away! For of this sort are those who creep into households and make captives of gullible women loaded down with sins, led away by various lusts, always learning and never able to come to the knowledge of the truth. Now as Jannes and Jambres resisted Moses, so do these also resist the truth: men of corrupt minds, disapproved concerning the faith; but they will progress no further, for their folly will be manifest to all, as theirs also was. But you have carefully followed my doctrine, manner of* *life, purpose, faith, longsuffering, love, perseverance, persecutions, afflictions, which happened to me at Antioch, at Iconium, at Lystra— what persecutions I endured. And out of them all the Lord delivered me. Yes, and all who desire to live godly in Christ Jesus will suffer persecution. But evil men and impostors will grow worse and worse, deceiving and being deceived. But you must continue in the things which you have learned and been assured of, knowing from whom you have learned them, and that from childhood you have known the Holy Scriptures, which are able to make you wise for salvation through faith which is in Christ Jesus. <u>All Scripture is given by inspiration of God, and is profitable for doctrine, for reproof, for correction, for instruction in righteousness, that the man of God may be complete, thoroughly equipped for every good work</u>".* (Emphasis mine)

Suggested Prayer for Deliverance and Salvation

Maybe you have never lead anyone in a prayer deliverance or Salvation before? The following prayer, that I have used, is offered as a guide so that you may be aware of the things one should cover when leading someone to accept Jesus Christ into their lives and be set free from cultic and occultic bondage:

"Lord Jesus Christ, I believe you died for me on the Cross at Calvary for the sins of mankind and for my personal sins and that you rose again from the dead. You redeemed me by your shed Blood and I want to belong to you. I confess all my sins – (name those that come to mind) – I'm sorry for them all. I forgive all others as I want you to forgive me. Forgive me now and cleanse me with your Blood. I thank you for the Blood of Jesus Christ which cleanses me from all sin. I now come to you as my deliverer. You know my special needs, the thing that binds, the thing that torments, that defiles, that evil spirit, that unclean spirit -(the deceiving spirit behind the cult/group you've been involved with- name the cult/group!) – I renounce and bind it and I command it to get out of my life (and family?) and stay out in Jesus' Name! I claim the promise of your Word that, "Whoever calls on the name of the Lord Shall be saved." I call upon you now. In the name of the Lord Jesus Christ, please deliver me and set me free. Satan, I renounce you and all of your works. I loose myself from you, in the Name of Jesus and I command you to leave me right now, in Jesus' Name. Amen"!

CHAPTER THIRTEEN

Extra-Biblical Revelation

What is common to most cults is that they have and rely upon what is termed 'extra-Biblical revelation'. By that I mean they have adopted additional writings, which they believe is akin to Scripture, which they consider to be even more important than the Bible. Such writings are revered as being more recent and up to date than the Bible!

For instance, the Church of Jesus Christ of Latter Day Saints (the 'Mormons') have such publications in, "The Book of Mormon", "The Pearl of Great Price", and their "Journal of Discourses" and many more writings. Our task therefore is to demonstrate to the cultist why God's Word to man, the Bible, is the one and only true source of knowledge over and above all such 'extra' works. We must be able to show why their works must be regarded deficient and therefore false.

Remember, Christians, who are truly Born-again of the Spirit of God, make it their business to know not only what they believe, but why they believe it! This is because they can then demonstrate solid evidence for the truth and finality of God's Word. Notice how the Apostle Peter used such evidence in Acts Chapter 2 on the Day of Pentecost in Jerusalem, when he addressed the crowd that were present on that day. He used the historicity of Christianity and the prophetical truth of Christianity as his evidence, in order to teach and highlight the truth.

Having said that, you may have become somewhat discouraged by thinking that you can't possibly learn and absorb all of the information that you perhaps will need to know? You may even be thinking that you haven't got the ability to learn how to deal and cope with this? Be encouraged and always remember that almost all of the early Christians were just ordinary folk like us, who developed the capacity with the help of God's Holy Spirit, to learn and preach the truth of God's Word. Even your writer failed English in his first year at high school (through his lack of interest and application!).

Make Sure You Know Your Own Faith Well

We must know not only what we believe, but why we believe it! Most Christians know to some degree WHAT they believe, e.g., the tenets of the Apostle's Creed, the Lord's Prayer and etc. But they do not know WHY they believe it! The cults logically, capitalize on such 'ignorance' which over time has proven to be of great advantage for them when seeking to sway and convert people to their way of thinking!

The cultist's chief point of attack is usually: "If you're a Christian, then why do you believe 'such and such'...?" Few cultists, however, can confuse a Christian who is versed in basic Biblical theology (don't be frightened by the word!). As the late Dr. Walter Martin said so appropriately, "The poison of cultism can be effectively combated by the antidote of sound doctrine". (The Kingdom of the Cults, p352). In dealing with the cults, it is WHY you believe something to be true that is perhaps the most helpful and important thing.

In preparation for confronting a cultist one needs to study the REAL thing, and not the counterfeit, of which you only need and overview! A good analogy is to remember that when the banks train their people to detect counterfeit currency, they do not let them study anything but the genuine article! This is to assist them to become so familiar with the genuine banknote that they have a better chance of spotting the counterfeit! The same holds true with God's Word the Bible. We, as Christians must become so familiar with the Bible that we are equipped to immediately recognize Satan's counterfeits by comparison.

Be Equipped with some Basic Apologetics

By the word 'apologetics' we mean to make "a reasoned argument defending a theory or doctrine" (Oxford Dictionary). The reader is encouraged to contemplate what is written by the apostle in 2nd Peter 3:14-18 in this regard:

"Therefore, beloved, looking forward to these things, be diligent to be found by Him in peace, without spot and blameless; and consider that the longsuffering of our Lord is salvation—as also our beloved brother Paul, according to the wisdom given to him, has written to you, as also in all his epistles, speaking in them of these things, in which are some things hard to understand, which un-taught and unstable people twist to their own destruction, as they do also the rest of the Scriptures. You therefore, beloved, since you know this beforehand, beware lest you also fall from your own steadfastness, being led away with the error of the wicked; but grow in the grace and knowledge of our Lord and Savior Jesus Christ. To Him be the glory both now and forever. Amen" And then in Jude 22-23: *"And on some have compassion, making a distinction; but others save with fear, pulling them out of the fire..."*

To use pat answers, packaged platitudes, or trite clichés makes for very poor witnessing tools to use against any non-Christian, especially a cultist! We have to understand ahead of time that when it comes to 'apologetics' (which simply means, 'to contend for and justify the exclusiveness of the Christian faith'), it will be slow going with them because most people are 'experientially oriented' and NOT 'intellectually or rationally oriented'.

We must try our best to communicate true knowledge lovingly and patiently. Please remember that reason can never replace what reason didn't put there in the first place! All the good reasoning in the world will be of absolutely no use against an emotional orientation! Most cultists have been 'programmed', or coerced, without realizing it, to believe as they do. They have NEVER been encouraged to reason things out for themselves! In actual fact, they are discouraged to do so, often to the point of threat, from using their own reasoning powers. In contrast, the Christian is encouraged to do his own studies and to reason and think for himself and discuss and share what he is learning with others Christians may lovingly correct him in his understanding if he is wrong.

You can expect most cultists to confront you with their perceived 'weaknesses and divisions' within the established Church. Many cult members take great delight in confronting Christians cynically about the existence of the large number of denominations and what seems to them as being divisions in Christendom. They will most likely say "Well, at least our group is united, but look at you, you are all divided, and can't agree among yourselves on exactly what you believe". A good response to such a statement is to remind the person that one valid reason for so many different denominations is simply one of geography! For example, as Christian people moved from their country of birth and with their family faith to another country, that eventually for many it became wise and expedient to administratively 'cut the apron strings' so to speak, with their former homeland headquarters. Often, as numbers grew, in order to comply with the law of the land they would adopt a new name, even perhaps becoming a large denomination in time!

So, in answering this and other such multitudinous accusations, we must be open and honest and never try to hide or make excuses for our own so-called weaknesses, but we should be prepared to humbly admit them. However, we must be quick to point out that even though many of the denominations do have some differences, they are only on what are mainly secondary issues. Such denominational distinctives, as stated before, in most cases have no bearing whatsoever on preventing a seeker from finding true Salvation.

Remember that the mainline denominations are united around the most important and basic issue of all, that the Lord Jesus Christ is 'God manifest in the flesh' and therefore part of the Triune Godhead – the Trinity of the Father, Son, and Holy Spirit!

Keep Some Basic Materials on Hand for Your Own Use

It may be helpful to keep some basic leaflets, or tracts, on hand. Not necessarily to give them to the cultist, but for your own information and to help you to gain deeper personal insights. It may help you to memorise some of the points they raise with you and allow them to perhaps be a track, for you to follow in order to speak consistently with a particular cult member. It would make what you say to them seem more credible if you can speak with authority, which you can only if you have done your 'homework'? Perhaps you should obtain some of the small booklets that have been written especially for the traditional door-knocking or street-corner cultists. If possible, try to get two types: Firstly, tracts which clearly point out the false teachings and errors of the most common cults like Jehovah's Witnesses, Mormons, Seventh-Day Adventists *et al.* Secondly, try and get some good positive tracts that explain and defend the true historic Christian Faith. They usually contain all the knowledge you need 'in a nutshell'.

Here's an approach that you may like to adopt. As most cultists will want to leave something with you to read or listen to, why not agree to take theirs, if they take yours? In our experience most cultists have responded to this, as they love to leave something with you so as to give them a reason to come back. Remember to be polite in the exchange.

My recommendation is that you emphasise to them that you are only *lending* your material to the cultist! Why? Because our past experience has shown that if you give something to them, it immediately becomes 'their property' and it is most likely to be totally ignored and thrown into the next rubbish bin they pass! I know, because I used to do that! However, from my experience, if you lend something to them, then whatever it is, it remains as 'your property' and most cultists will respect that, knowing they will have to return it to you! This allows and gives opportunity for their curiosity to be peaked by the leading of the Holy Spirit!

He will 'move' upon them in answer to your prayers and they will be 'drawn' to read the subject matter of what it was that you lent to them They may not look at it in front of another person from their group, but they will often do so when they get home and or in private. Always remember the old saying about human nature, "Curiosity killed the cat!"

Should you not be comfortable, or caught on the hop by a

cultist, take comfort in the following suggestions that may be simpler for you to use? Not wishing to 'reinvent the wheel', I quote from an article posted on the Christian Debaters website,[89] with the heading, "Understanding People in Cults". They conclude under the sub-heading, 'We Should Be A Mirror Of Christ To All' They go on to say, "It is not essential to win every argument; it is more important to win the person. We should be a mirror, in which the cultists can see how seriously their cult differs from what God taught as primary things in the Bible.

However, more importantly, we should mirror Christ, reflecting his Light. You should aim to do the following: Tell them it is important to seek the truth no matter what the cost. Following a lie does not please god. Tell them not just that God loves them, but tell them about the One True, Most High Living God, who loves them! Tell them not just that they are sinners, but there is no possible hope for them apart from Christ. Do not tell them Christ provided a way to god. Rather, tell them that Christ came from God and provided the one and only way, God's way to Himself. Tell them they must repent and accept the Jesus of the Bible, not just any Jesus, as their Lord and Savior. It is not as important to know all the answers as to know the one who is the Answer. You are free from having to worry about whether your knowledge or your clear presentation is good enough to win them to Christ, because if you try and do it in your own strength, it will never be good enough regardless of how much you study. Without prayer and without God working in their life, drawing them to the truth, their situation would be hopeless; Satan's

---

[89] http://www.biblequery.org/

deception is just too strong. So do not rely on yourself, but pray for them and for God's help, even despite your words and mistakes. As Paul said in 2nd Corinthians 12:10, "Therefore I take pleasure in infirmities, in reproaches, in needs, in persecutions, in distresses, for Christ's sake. For when I am weak, then I am strong.".

CHAPTER FOURTEEN

Some Probing Questions for the Cultist

With diligent preparation it will enable you to take the offensive position when the cultist calls, or you confront a cult member. This means you can, without it being obvious, control the flow and direction of the conversation. Remember that the cultist is on your 'home turf' or territory. Which means you are the one with the advantage and have the authority! All cult members are trained by their leaders to respect and be obedient to authority and they will mostly respect yours.

For example. Many years ago, two Mormons knocked at our front door. I listened to them and asked a couple of relevant questions to which they politely listended and responded. Knowing that they were keen to move on, I felt to let them go but I invited them to visit with us at 7pm two nights later. When they arrived only one of the original two was present. I still invited them in. After exchanging pleasantries, the one I did not invite was obviously the more experienced of the two, who I believe had come along to "put me in my place"!

He tried to lead and dominate the discussion from the start. However, to quieten him down I said, "Excuse me, but I didn't invite you to come tonight. You've obviously invited yourself. I invited your friend here and the one who was with him when they first called. So would you please sit quietly and allow me to continue my discussion with the person that I did invite!" He apologized to me and sat there and said very little until it came time to say our goodbyes later in the evening! He had to 'endure' listening to the interesting discussion that I had with his colleague!

Listed below are some suggested questions to think about which may be of help to get you started. They are, of course, 'loaded' Christian questions, you may come across others just a good:

(a) What scholarship and research is the basis for your Biblical interpretation?

(b) What other nationally, or internationally qualified and recognized Bible scholars agree with your scriptural exegesis (or, explanation)?

(c) What other sacred writings do you believe in, other than the Bible?

(d) Who is it that checks out your founder/leader?

(e) To whom is your leader accountable to and to whom does he/she have to answer to?

(f) Why does your leader say they are accountable and responsible to no one other than Jesus, or God?

(g) What authority therefore is your leadership under, other than his or her own?

(h) What do you see as the essential difference between the teachings of your group and that of the established church?

(j) What does your group's theology, philosophy, or teaching offer me that I do not already have as a Christian?

(k) Are those who are in your group the only people on earth who are going to be saved? If so, what do you believe will ultimately happen to me if I don't accept and follow your group's teachings? (This can be a most embarrassing question for many cultists as they won't want to tell you so 'up front' as they many cults really believe that you will die if you don't join with them!)

(l) For me to be saved would I have to quit my local church and join with your group?

(m) What is your view of the church as a whole today?

(n) What do you believe a person has to do to have an abundant life here on earth and be assured of eternal life with God in the life to come?

(o) Do you feel that your group is the only true preacher or interpreter of the Gospel today?

(p) Of all of the other religious groups in the world, is your group alone the only enlightened one? If not, who are other notable Christian or religious groups that you recognize as also teaching truth and are equal with you in your enlightenment and understanding?

(q) What is the nature of God?

(r) Who is the Holy Spirit?

(s) What is your understanding of sin?

(t) Do you believe that man is a sinner by nature? If you don't, then what is your explanation for man's current plight? Then, if you do believe that man is a sinner by nature, what is the means of receiving atonement, or forgiveness, for that sin?

(u) Why do you not believe that the Lord Jesus Christ alone is the answer to your needs and to the needs of the world?

As one's knowledge of the Bible and the false teachings of the cults increases, one will find that there are many other important questions that could be added to the foregoing list.

God's plan for enlarging His kingdom is so simple - one person telling another about the Savior. Yet we're busy and full of excuses. Just remember, someone's eternal destiny is at stake. The joy you'll have when you meet that person in heaven will far exceed any discomfort you felt in sharing the gospel.
-Charles Stanley

CHAPTER FIFTEEN

CONFRONTING THE CULTIST

You should always begin your encounter with prayer as you are about to enter into a spiritual battle! You should of course always take the time to exchange pleasantries and not go 'straight for the jugular' so to speak. If you don't know the person/s then make the time to get to know something about them. Always thank them for the opportunity to share with them and tell them you are happy to listen to what they have to say. Then, once you are all settled you can perhaps do the following.

As mentioned make sure you are prepared prayerfully beforehand. Pray with them, or in spite of them, whenever it is possible. It's best not to even ask them for permission to pray, as you may give them an opportunity to say "No"! Remember, they are on your turf and you are the one with authority. You could begin by saying something like the following:

"Well, I never like to discuss things about God or Bible matters without first talking to Him about it. So let's pray and ask for God's wisdom and blessing upon our discussion". Then, ignoring any arising protestations, IMMEDIATELY begin to pray out loud! Remember, they will invariably decline to pray with you if you offer them the opportunity, but there are very few people in this world who will attempt to interrupt another person who is praying, regardless of how much they may disagree with their beliefs.

When you are praying in front a cultist, try if you know how, to be sensitive to the terminology that you use in addressing God, especially if it's a Jehovah's Witness! In their case, you could begin your prayer by addressing "Yahweh God" (note that the word *'jehovah'* is of late medieval origin and is a false translation of God's name and it means absolutely nothing in Hebrew![90]) You can thank God that He has revealed Himself totally in the person of His only Son, Jesus Christ. You can thank God in your prayers for His Holy Spirit to lead in your discussion – why? Because it's the Holy Spirit's job to guide and lead a person into all truth (see John 16:13). If you have time, you could pray that the truth of God's Word would prevail in the conversation. Beginning with prayer gives you an opportunity to subtly set the tone for the conversation and to say some things about God and Christ that would be difficult to have said otherwise.

Establish Some Common Ground

Before entering into your prepared discussion with a cultist, you should try to establish some common ground with them, preferably the inspiration and authority of Scriptures, the Bible. If this is not possible, then try to establish the personality of God - that He is an actual being and not some impersonal all-pervading 'force', or 'energy' somewhere in the Universe.

For example, you could refer to John 14:6-11 and highlight what Jesus said to Philip in answer to his question in Verse 8: *"Lord, show us the Father, and it is sufficient for us."* You

---

[90] "Jehovah" is actually a hybridization of a German transliteration of a mixed up collection of Hebrew consonants and vowels.

could also refer to the use of personal pronouns, such as *"He"* and *"Him"* which are used in Verses 16-17 and again in Chapter 16:13-14 for the Holy Spirit.

We need to do this because most cultists, especially the Jehovah's Witnesses and the Mormons[91], come armed with briefcases full of their own literature, with which they are better versed than the average Christian. Try to get them to agree and even challenge them to stick to the Bible alone in your discussion! By doing this you will be confining yourself to the 'primary' source, not some other 'secondary' source, or some other so-called 'inspired' work.

When quoting from or reading from the Bible, make sure that you use a translation that is widely recognized and accepted. One that is used by the church at large. For example, the King James Version, New King James Version, Revised Standard Version, New International Version, and etc. This is especially true in the case of the 'translation' used by the Jehovah's Witnesses, *The New World Translation*, which has been deceitfully altered by their leaders to conform to their own peculiar and unique teachings! If you do want to use the JW's version, then try to get to know its weaknesses and inaccuracies ahead of time. Most good Christian bookstores stock materials[92] regarding the errors of the cults, or they can easily order them in for you. You could also visit our Website and under the heading 'Facts About' view the article about their 'bible translation' titled, 'The World's Most Dangerous Book'.

---

[91] Mormons belong to 'The Church of Jesus Christ of Latter-Day Saints'
[92] Things like leaflets, pamphlets, booklets, books, CDs and DVDs

Finally, be careful NOT to get caught up in the practice of quoting isolated scriptures, or 'proof texts' (which are often taken out of context) as many cults who use the Bible do. If you accept their 'proof texts' there is a good chance that you will only finish up chasing 'theological rabbits' down bottomless burrows! Most cultists are masters at using isolated texts from the Bible. Consequently, they often quote verses out of context to try to prove their points. Remember, any Scripture that is taken out context, automatically becomes a pretext![93] Many a 'shaky' Christian lacking knowledge has been won to a cult by using the ploy of keeping him away from the fundamental and core issues of the true Christian faith.

Be Careful about Your Attitude

On the one hand, don't have an attitude of timidity and inferiority. The Apostle Paul advises us in two parts of Scripture how we should conduct ourselves. Firstly, we should not be fearful, *"For God has not given us a spirit of fear, but of power and of love and of a sound mind"* (2nd Timothy 1:7). Then secondly and on the other hand, we should not adopt an attitude of pride and superiority, *"Now I, Paul, myself am pleading with you by the meekness and gentleness of Christ—who in presence am lowly among you...For though we walk in the flesh, we do not war according to the flesh. For the weapons of our warfare are not carnal but mighty in God for pulling down strong-holds, casting down arguments and every high thing that exalts itself against the knowledge of God, bringing every thought into captivity to the obedience of Christ..."* (2nd Corinthians 10:1).

---

[93] A 'pretext' is a reason given in justification of a course of action that is not the real reason.

From the beginning of your discussion, do everything possible that you can to make the person feel relaxed and comfortable. Try not to put them on the defensive. An attitude of real friendliness and sincerity can go a long way in disarming a cultist because he is usually prejudiced and defensive towards all Christians from the outset, usually because of their past bad experiences in church, or with church leaders.

A good way to disarm a cultist is to simply ask them to tell you about themselves, then just sit and listen. Questions regarding their marital status, number of children they may have, what they do for work, and similar are all good conversation starters. Don't forget to take time to acknowledge the good things that are in their life and commend them for those practices that you believe are exemplary.

For example and if appropriate, commend them for their their zeal, their dedication, their sacrifice of time and money and so on. Remember how wise the Apostle Paul was when he addressed the distinguished men of the Council of Athens on the hill of the Aeropagus? He said, *"I perceive that in every way you are very religious"* (Acts 17:22). He didn't begin his discourse by saying something like, "You great rotten bunch of idolatrous heathens, if you don't accept Christ, you're all going to finish up in hell!" Not the way to go. Please try to be loving and positive in your approach – you will find that it works wonders and is less stressful for both you and for them!

Most importantly, we really are obligated to reach out to them in true *'agape'* (selfless) love, which will show them a practical desire to help kind of love. Some call it 'Selfless Love'. Love is also a 'Fruit of the Holy Spirit' – see Galatians 5:22-23.

We should always seek to befriend them if it is possible

and try to establish a relationship with them. That will help to drive a wedge into their beliefs as initially they will see you as an 'enemy' to be won. Better to be a friend to know. Make sure that you see them as human beings who have been created in the image of God. They should not see us as infidels who need to have their spiritual heads lopped off!

Remember, most cult people have found in their belief system a particular fellowship that was perhaps lacking in their previous church or family experience. They may have found degrees of personal and social acceptance that they have perhaps never known in their lives before. Therefore, as Christians, if we are going to reach them for Christ, we are going to have to show them a degree of love, warmth, interest, concern and acceptance that is at least as great as, or possibly even greater than that which they have experienced from their particular cult or group.

So, if you really love them with the 'Jesus kind of love', it really will drive that important wedge into their thinking. Because, in their minds they will begin to think, "How can this person be such a friendly and loving person and not share in my beliefs?" or, "How can this person accept me as he has and yet seem so kind and still reject my beliefs?" They could even be thinking, as many have done, "This person would make a good member of our cult or group?"

Remember, cultists who claim to be Christian have been coerced with the idea by their leaders that anyone who opposes their beliefs has to be motivated by the Devil. So your loving attitude towards them will go a long way towards destroying, or casting doubts on his beliefs and learned prejudices towards you.

Finally, be firm with them, but at the same time be tender. Under no circumstances should you compromise God's Truth!

Rather, as the Bible counsels, speak the truth to them in love (Ephesians 3:15). Above all, don't try be so tactful that you may tend to stretch the truth, or be so ruthlessly truthful that you are not loving. Through your own time of Bible reading and prayer, bathe God's trut h with God's love and then when given the opportunity, speak it in love.

In Your Discussion Always Stick to Key Issues

It is most important that you to stick to the person, nature and work of Jesus Christ. Never allow yourself to be conned into chasing those 'theological rabbits' that I have already mentioned! As your conversation progresses, make sure that you have the person define all his terms and to give the basis of his authority for that definition. The following words or phrases are suggested as being valid questions that need to be carefully defined:

- What is meant by the 'Deity of Christ'?
- What is meant by 'Justification'?
- What is meant by the 'Incarnation'?
- Where will one spend 'Eternity'?
- What does it mean for one to be 'Born-again'?
- What are the two 'Judgments' about?
- What is a 'False Prophet'?
- What is a 'False Christ'?
- Is it important to understand the Resurrection?

If you find these questions daunting, then you will probably need to find a friendly and sincere Christian to help you to understand what significance these questions have and how important their answers to them really are. If you are up to it, you could contact your nearest recognized evangelical church, Christian bookstore, or even contact us through our website as we may be able to help you find one who can help.

Concerning the Lord Jesus Christ, you should not only deal with the importance of His sacrificial and atoning death on the Cross of Calvary (which reconciled man to God), but also the importance of His physical resurrection from the dead. You might ask them questions like: "Why was it so important to His followers that Jesus Christ was physically resurrected from the dead?" The answer is found in 1st Corinthians 15:13-17 which says: *"But if there is no resurrection of the dead, then Christ is not risen. And if Christ is not risen, then our preaching is empty and your faith is also empty. Yes, and we are found false witnesses of God, because we have testified of God that He raised up Christ, whom He did not raise up—if in fact the dead do not rise. For if the dead do not rise, then Christ is not risen. And if Christ is not risen, your faith is futile; you are still in your sins!"*

After reading this, you could perhaps add, "Well, we both know that Buddha is dead (Buddhism), Mohammed is dead (Islam), Ellen G. White (SDA) is dead, Joseph Smith Junior (Mormons) is dead, and one day your leader will also be die (if this has not already been the case?). Naturally, you may be sad about it, but have you ever asked the question, "Is there any valid reason for him/her to rise again from the dead?" After asking that question, give them some time to answer, which they can't. Then you could say, "You'll find there isn't one because you have already received all of his/her so-called 'light', or 'revelation', and even now you have it with you." You could then ask, "So why was the resurrection of Jesus Christ so important to His disciples?"

Identify the Past Spiritual Vacuums in Their Life

This can best be done by asking the cultist what was it that actually drew him/her in the first place, into his particular group? Ask if they he had an involvement in a church before joining their present group. If they did, then ask which church it was and why they left it? We have found that most will be only too happy to share about things like this! Their answers will give you a good opportunity and insight to be able to understand their background as it is important to know what they may have once believed. This approach enables you to find out what their needs were back then and can help you to identify the spiritual vacuum that may still exist in their lives that set them up as candidates for a cult.

Once you've asked a question, always give them an honest and fair opportunity to answer it so they can explain their views without being constantly interrupted. Don't be so preoccupied with thinking about what your next response is going to be that you don't really listen to what they are saying. Listening is quite an art and can be difficult to learn and one that the writer has had to work hard on over the years – I still find I have to restrain myself at times from 'jumping in' when a cultist says something that I know is incorrect!

Please remember, that the first and most important part of witnessing to anyone is to listen! We have to try to understand what they think and what they believe, if we are ever going to have a chance of being able to help them. If you honestly and sincerely hear them out, they will more than likely do the same for you when it is your turn to speak. Quite often, if you find it hard to get a word in edgewise, the writer has learned to say to the cultist, "Excuse me, I listened to what you had to say and now I believe that now you must be willing to allow me the same courtesy." This tactic has never failed to get the conversation back on track! Try not to forget what we said about them 'being on your turf', as it means that you have authority. So, be loving and gentle in how you exercise it.

Don't be fooled by any experiences they may claim to have had. Never ever forget that the devil is able to counterfeit all of the gifts of the Holy Spirit, with the exception of one, the Discerning of Spirits[94] (1st Corinthians 12:4-11), and that he is the master of the art of 'counterfeit experiences'. So don't try to tear down or belittle any of their experiences. Why? Because their experiences are just as real to them as your own experiences were to you. Remember, the cultist has invariably experienced something, even though it may have been the counterfeit!

In one of our discussions, the local Transcendental Meditation (TM) teacher kept referring to experience as being a 'proof' by saying: "Well, all I can say is that all of the people I know who practice TM are experiencing something"!

It was very obvious from my own experience and likewise with many that we've spoken to over the years, that when we first joined a cult we did initially experience a degree of peace and tranquility because we all felt that we had found answers for our immediate problems. Someone commented the other day that when someone leaves a Christian church to join with cult, which claims to be Christian, the person thinks he has left a 'false church' and joined with a true Christian church!

The Lord Jesus tells us: *"Peace I leave with you, My peace I give to you; not as the world gives do I give to you. Let not your heart be*

---

[94] The devil's counterfeit of the gift of discernment, which he cannot use is the knowledge of his cohorts known as 'Familiar Spirits'

troubled, neither let it be afraid." (John 14:27). Notice that he infers that there is a 'worldly peace' that people can receive, but it is a peace that comes by none other than the Father of Lies - Satan! If you were to say: "Well, I've found peace in Christ" then the cultist will more than likely answer you by responding "I've found I've really been searching for through learning to practice TM"; "...since I gained Krishna Consciousness"; "...through practicing Yoga"; "...since I became a Seventh-Day Adventist"; ...since becoming a Jehovah's Witness, *et al.* We should never fall into the trap of swapping spiritual experiences, because most cults are very experientially oriented, so a discussion based around experiences tends to go nowhere fast.

It is of great importance to stay with the historic Biblical understanding and revelation of God in Christ. You could point out to them that all of your experiences are based upon historical, objective, and propositional truth. A good principle to remember is that all valid experience is derived from truth, and never the reverse! We must always test our experiences against truth and we should never try to infer a truth from our experience.

Check Their Attitude Toward Sin

You should check with them and find out what their attitude toward sin is, both in the world and in their personal life? You could ask them how they realistically deal with evil in general? Or, how do they intend to deal with personal sin in their own life? Their inadequate understanding, and often very low view of sin and retribution, can be revealed by discussing with them the reason for Christ's death on the Cross.
Very few cultic groups have a clear understanding of the meaning

of what actually took place at Calvary. For example, members of Islam[95] and the Bahá'ís[96] may accept Jesus Christ as being a 'manifestation of god', but they have absolutely no clear understanding of the meaning and purpose of His sacrificial and atoning death upon the Cross!

A reminder that you can use this gap in their understanding and ask the question, "Why do you think it was necessary for Christ to die as he did?" Their answer to this question will quickly reveal their understanding of the nature of man and his condition before God, as well as what they feel is the solution to mankind's problems. The answer of course is that He died because it paved the only true way for the Salvation of mankind and mankind's reconciliation to God! Even though many religious people and cultists believe that it was not necessary for Christ to die on the Cross, it is easy to point out to them from Scripture that this was Jesus' own conviction and reason for His coming to earth! In Matthew 16:21 it states, *"From that time Jesus began to show to His disciples that He must go to Jerusalem, and suffer many things from the elders and chief priests and scribes, and be killed, and be raised the third day". l Him, and the third day He will be raised up." And they were exceedingly sorrowful"*.

---

[95] According to Islam, Jesus never died on the Cross, nor ever wanted to die on the Cross, nor ever was born to die on the Cross.

[96] They believe as follows: Throughout history, God has revealed Himself through a succession of Divine Messengers, Whose teachings—moral, spiritual, and social—have renewed man's relationship to God and provided the basis for the advancement of human society. Among them have been Abraham, Krishna, Zoroaster, Moses, Buddha, Jesus, Muhammad, the Báb, and Bahá'u'lláh, as well as other Teachers whose names have been lost or obscured over time..." http://www.bahai.org/faq/ Accessed 19 May 2014

CHAPTER SIXTEEN

Some Do's and Don'ts

Do try to share your personal Christian testimony. When sharing your faith with others, you should try to emphasize the all-sufficiency of Jesus Christ in your own life. Tell them how confident and assured you are concerning your present Christian inheritance. Very few cultists will profess that they have the assurance of eternal life now and have true peace with God. This lack of assurance accounts for much of their zeal and activity because they have been taught that it is only by their own efforts, or works, that they can secure their salvation and have assurance before God. True salvation is not through works but by faith and the grace and mercy of God, just as the Bible teaches. If the opportunity arises, you could read to them Scripture verses like those following: *"...I am not ashamed, for I know whom I have believed and am persuaded that He is able to keep what I have committed to Him until that Day"*. 2nd Timothy 1:12

"Therefore, having been justified by faith, we have peace with God through our Lord Jesus Christ, through whom also we have access by faith into this grace in which we stand, and rejoice in hope of the glory of God". Romans 5:1-2

"In Him you also trusted, after you heard the word of truth, the gospel of your salvation; in whom also, having believed, you were sealed with the Holy Spirit of promise, who is the guarantee of our inheritance until the redemption of the purchased possession, to the praise of His glory". Ephesians 1:13-14

Don't Be Put Off by Hostility or Antagonism

Some cult members, when challenged, can often become very hostile or irritated towards anyone who dares to question or oppose their beliefs. Some, like the JW's and Mormons will even try to frustrate and trap you in order to make you lose your own peace. Many have shared with me that they have lost it in this area because they were simply not adequately prepared when they called!

Therefore, it is crucial that you always operate with "...*the mind of Christ*" (1st Corinthians 2:16) and that you behave as a Christian and not allow yourself to be ruled by your emotions. When you cease to operate with a Spirit-guided mind, you will inevitably begin to operate with fleshly emotionalism which only results in heated arguments, belligerence, and even name-calling!

Most importantly, a good thing to remember is not to refer to their cult leaders, or founders, as being 'false prophets' or 'false christs' even if you know that they truthfully are! Remember that if you feel yourself getting a bit 'overheated' with them then simply have the grace to apologize to them – they will respect you for it. Paul counsels us, *"Let your speech always be with grace, seasoned with salt, that you may know how you ought to answer each one"* (*Colossians 4:6*).

If You Can't Win Them Do At Least Warn Them

Over time, if you don't succeed in convincing them of their error, then you MUST in love, warn them of the judgement of God that will come upon their error and upon all perversions of His True Gospel. Remember, the words of the Apostle Paul, *"Him we preach, warning every man and teaching every man in all wisdom, that we may present every man perfect in Christ Jesus. To this end I also labour, striving according to His working which works in me mightily"* (Colossians 1:28).

The prophet Ezekiel also warns in 33:8-9, *"When I say to the wicked, 'O wicked man, you shall surely die!' and you do not speak to warn the wicked from his way, that wicked man shall die in his iniquity; but his blood I will require at your hand. Nevertheless if you warn the wicked to turn from his way, and he does not turn from his way, he shall die in his iniquity; but you have delivered your soul".*

Paul advises again in Titus 3:10-11 that we should avoid where possible the creating of dissension, *"But avoid foolish disputes, genealogies, contentions, and strivings about the law; for they are unprofitable and useless. Reject a divisive man after the first and second admonition, knowing that such a person is warped and sinning, being self-condemned".* He also warned those who were preaching 'another gospel', *"...but there are some who trouble you and want to pervert the gospel of Christ. But even if we, or an angel from heaven, preach any other gospel to you than what we have preached to you, let him be accursed"* Galatians 1:8

Thank Them for Coming

Before they leave, remember to thank them for coming and for allowing you to share your faith in Christ with them. If you think it may be appropriate, pray again before they leave. You could say something like, "Well we've discussed a lot of things today and I think it would be fitting if we were to close our discussion with prayer". Then, do as you did at the beginning and immediately begin to pray!

If they are willing, obtain their name and phone number, so that that you can follow them up soon after their visit. Perhaps in exchange for their literature (if they should offer you any), you could possibly lend them some of those good tracts and pamphlets, that I mentioned earlier to take with them to further define, explain and defend your faith.

If you time has gone really well, you could even lend them a good modern translation of the Bible or New Testament to take with them – most Christian bookstores have stocks of cheaper paperback Bibles and New Testaments. If they are hesitant, you could challenge them with something like: "Well, if you have really found the truth, as you have told me, then it cannot hurt you to read this. You owe it to yourself to examine all the evidence since it is your soul that hangs in the balance!"

The writer usually concludes a discussion, where there seems to be no headway made, by adding, "Well, both of us can't be right, one of us must be absolutely dead wrong. I've taken the time to read and study about your organization, or group. I know its history, I know about its founder, and his writings and I am convinced that it is in error! So I do hope you will take this information and objectively study it in the privacy of your own home. I would also ask that you show me where you think it is wrong. Why you may ask? Because, it could make the difference as to where you will spend Eternity!"

You should also assure them that you have not meant to personally offend them in any way during your discussion, even though you strongly reject their beliefs; that you still have nothing but love for them as a person. If you feel confident enough, invite them back for further discussion, particularly in reference to obtaining their opinion of the material you may have just lent to them.

After They Leave – Evaluate Your Encounter

As soon as they leave, while everything is still fresh in your mind, evaluate for a few moments your encounter. Perhaps jot down some notes, in particular any areas where you felt you were not strong in explaining or defending your faith. It is especially important that you allow these encounters to become your own personal learning and strengthening experience.

You should write down any questions that you were confronted with that stumped you or perhaps even confused you at the time. When you have done so, make the time to do your research and get the answers you need. If you fail to do this, you might eventually lose your confidence about having further encounters with cult members. If you do lose your confidence then Satan and his minions will have won another victory!

Follow Them Up – After All, It's Your Responsibility

Put them on your prayer list and specifically pray for them daily, just as you would for any other person that you have had the opportunity to share Christ with. Take the initiative to make the effort to follow them up in as many ways as you can. Don't just sit at home and wonder when, or if, they might ever call again. Remember, if they approached you first, that it was they who took the initiative for the first encounter, so why not take the initiative for the second, or follow-up encounter!

Your follow-up may take the form of a telephone conversation, or a personal visit. When you speak or meet, remember to thank them again for visiting you and at the same time, re-issue an invitation to have further discussions. If they are open to it, you could arrange to obtain for them some additional Christian literature. This may be agreed to one-on-one as usually they will not commit to such an offer while another of their group is present. If they accept your offer it will continue to challenge their beliefs, as well as be a witness of the truth of the Gospel to them. If, as mentioned, they stumped you with questions you could not answer on the day, be sure to do your homework by finding answers for them. This usually accomplishes two things. Firstly, it will let them know that you believe in your faith and care enough to go to the trouble of finding and getting an answer just for them. Secondly, it will alleviate any delusions that they might have taken home with them about thinking they had successfully refuted another 'dumb' Christian once again!

From the writer's own experience, during my early weeks of being associated with Jehovah's Witness, I remember the following experience vividly, even today! It occurred on my very first day of apprehensively going out to knock on doors with the JW's in what they call 'Field Service'. I was partnered with an elder named Gerry – his task was to teach me how it was done.

When we came to our very first house, I opened the front gate as instructed and I walked up the path following Gerry, climbed several steps; crossed the veranda to the front door. I had been instructed to say nothing, other than a 'Hello', and just listen and observe. Gerry had asked me to knock and I did. A few seconds later, a woman opened the door and my Gerry said, "Good morning, we are Jehovah's Witnesses and we are ..." That was as far as he got! The woman cut him off and loudly said, "Well, I have my own religion, I'm a Christian so get the hell out of here!" and slammed the door in our faces!

As we walked the path to the gate, Gerry said, 'There you are, that's what I've been telling you about people outside Jehovah's Organisation. If that woman was a genuine Christian she would never have spoken to us like she did. She wouldn't have slammed the door in our face either." I'm afraid that I had to agree with him on that one! I remember thinking that maybe what the JW's had been teaching me was really true? Maybe those churches I had been going to in my life did not really have 'the Truth'[97]

However, it was what happened on my very next outing that really convinced me that by being with the JW's was the right place to be! I was again with Gerry, and as we walked up the driveway to an open garage, in which a man was working on his car, we said good morning to him and again my partner respectfully introduced us. The man responded by saying that he was a Christian and served as an Elder in his local church. Without batting an eye, Gerry launched into his rehearsed presentation about the then controversial war in Vietnam and all the other conflicts and problems going on in the world were signs that we were living in the time of the End!

What then occurred stunned me just like the woman I mentioned before. The poor man was so rattled by the conversation that he started to tremble and his responses were all over the place! I noticed that his saliva gathered at the corners of his lips and it wasn't long before he soon told us to leave and closed the garage door!

Again, as we walked away Gerry said, "There you are my brother, just another example for you to see how ignorant those who claim to be Christians really are. That man said he was an

---

[97] Jehovah's Witnesses believe that they are the only ones who have 'the Truth' and that all others who claim to be 'Christian' belong to, 'Babylon the Great – The World Empire of False Religion' – which they believe is headed up by the Roman Catholic Church and that all Protestant Churches were simply 'Daughters of Rome'!

elder in his church and did not know how to defend his so-called faith!" I responded, "Yes, for an elder he was pretty weak wasn't he?" What did the woman and man I encountered do for me? Their reactions and those of many others that I met over the next few years had the effect of confirming and convincing me that I was on the right track by joining with the JW's!

I've had many ex-JW's and those who have left other 'christian' cults, tell me the same thing, that it was the reaction to the actions of those who opposed and abused them verbally, and even physically, that helped to 'cement' them into their cult group just as it was for me!

Remember, that God's desire is that none should be lost and that all should come to repentance and be saved.[98] Therefore we, as true Christians are obligated to be loving and careful when we are confronted by those who represent 'another (false) gospel'. Remember, through our own ignorance and our wrong reactions we may, without realising it, be actually confirming to deceived people, who approach us representing a 'false gospel', that (in their minds) that they are in the right place spiritually with the cult they have are associated with!

---

[98] 2nd Peter 3:9

ANSWER TO THE CULT EXPLOSION

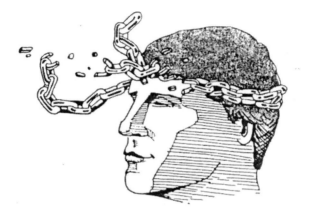

The Battleground Is In The Mind – Only The Truth Of God's Word Can Break The Chains of Bondage

STEPS TO SPIRITUAL MATURITY

"...for this very reason, giving all diligence, add to your faith virtue, to virtue knowledge, to knowledge self-control, to self-control perseverance, to perseverance godliness, to godliness brotherly kindness, and to brotherly kindness love. For if these things are yours and abound, you will be neither barren nor unfruitful in the knowledge of our Lord Jesus Christ. For he who lacks these things is shortsighted, even to blindness, and has forgotten that he was cleansed from his old sins. Therefore, brethren, be even more diligent to make your call and election sure, for if you do these things you will never stumble; for so an entrance will be supplied to you abundantly into the everlasting kingdom of our Lord and Saviour Jesus Christ." 1st Peter 1:3-11

CHAPTER SEVENTEEN

Scriptural Steps to Set People Free

The following Scriptural steps should not be entered into casually. Effort, diligence and time are required to become reasonably competent to have any chance of achieving the result that you want. If you are not prepared to give of yourself whole-heartedly to learning, then now is the time to withdraw as you may do more harm than good. However, if it is your heart's desire to set someone free in Jesus' Name who is lost in a cultic false religious system, then be prepared for a blessing in God's timing!

The First Step Is To Recognise That You Need Help!

You cannot proceed in your own strength successfully. You have to recognize and accept that fact that you need help and some training. Remember that you are not alone in your task. Look up the following verses from your own Bible, highlight and become familiar with them. Yes, you CAN do all things in Christ's strength as Philippians 4:13 says, *"I can do all things through Christ who strengthens me".*

In the following paragraph, I am going to outline for you, in perhaps a different way, the way in which Jesus himself spoke to a very religious man, about the reasons why it is imperative for us to be Born-again. If you have already been Born-again, then you may use the following reasoning to help others. If you are not yet Born-again, then you need to take it on-board personally, and then when the occasion arises, you can share it with another who needs to have Jesus in their life too!

If you belong to the Lord Jesus Christ as a result of being Born-again, then you are not alone in your endeavour to help your loved ones, or friends, who may be already in a cult, or becoming involved with one. Notice the substance of the conversation Jesus had with a very religious man named Nicodemus, in John 3:1-7:

"There was a man of the Pharisees named Nicodemus, a ruler of the Jews. This man came to Jesus by night and said to Him, "Rabbi, we know that you are a teacher come from God; for no one can do these signs that you do unless God is with him." Jesus answered and said to him, "Most assuredly, I say to you, unless one is born again, he <u>cannot see</u> the kingdom of God." Nicodemus said to Him, "How can a man be born when he is old? Can he enter a second time into his mother's womb and be born?" Jesus answered, "Most assuredly, I say to you, unless one is born of water and the Spirit, he <u>cannot enter</u> the kingdom of God. That which is born of the flesh is flesh, and that which is born of the Spirit is spirit. Do not marvel that I said to you, 'You must be born again.'"
(Bolding and underlining added)

If you are not sure that you are 'Born-again' or 'Saved' as many would say, you can avail yourself of this 'new birth' as a free gift from God, which is mentioned in Ephesians 2:8-9:

"For by grace you have been saved through faith, and that not of

yourselves; it is the gift of God, not of works, lest anyone should boast. For we are His workmanship, created in Christ Jesus for good works, which God prepared beforehand that we should walk in them".

You can do this for yourself by prayerfully taking the following steps[99]:

<u>Step 1:</u> Repent (means to be truly sorry) and turn away from doing the things that you really know deep-down are wrong, *"Repent therefore and be converted, that your sins may be blotted out, so that times of refreshing may come from the presence of the Lord"* (Acts 3:19-20)

<u>Step 2:</u> Then believe and confess Jesus Christ as your Lord, *"But what does it say? "The word is near you, in your mouth and in your heart" (that is, the word of faith which we preach): that if you confess with your mouth the Lord Jesus and believe in your heart that God has raised Him from the dead, you will be saved. For with the heart one believes unto righteousness, and with the mouth confession is made unto salvation. For the Scripture says, "Whoever believes on Him will not be put to shame."* (Romans 10:8-11)

<u>Step 3:</u> Then receive (ask) Jesus Christ to come into your life and be both your Saviour and your Lord, *"But as many as received Him, to them He gave the right to become children of God, to those who believe in His name: who were born, not of blood, nor of the will of the flesh, nor of the will of man, but of God"* (John 1:12-13).

To become truly effective not only in your own life and to be basically equipped to share the Gospel with others, you must have the Holy Spirit operating in and through your life. I again

---

[99] For another approach in presenting or receiving the Gospel please see *"The Test"* in the Appendices

emphasize that this is only possible if you have first become a 'spiritual person' by the act of being Born-again. Just as being Born-again is an essential free gift, so too, is inviting the Holy Spirit to come into your life an essential free gift also!

<u>Step 4</u>: Prayerfully ask your Heavenly Father for the Holy Spirit to come into your life, *"...how much more will your heavenly Father give the Holy Spirit to those who ask Him!"* (Luke 11:13). The Holy Spirit's ministry is to guide you into the truth found in the Bible,
"However, when He, the Spirit of truth, has come, He will guide you into all truth; for He will not speak on His own authority, but whatever He hears He will speak; and He will tell you things to come. He will glorify Me, for He will take of what is Mine and declare it to you. All things that the Father has are Mine. Therefore I said that He will take of Mine and declare it to you" (John 16:13-15).

Be Prepared for a Spiritual Battle!

When confronting a cultist, or being confronted, by one, don't forget that you are always in a spiritual battle, not only for the other person's soul, but for your own protection. Your enemy, the devil and his demons are spirit beings and are only capable being overcome and their influence defeated by using spiritual weapons! Ephesians 6:10-17 reveals just what you are up against, for it says:

"Finally, my brethren, be strong in the Lord and in the power of His might. Put on the whole armour of God that you may be able to stand against the wiles of the devil. For we do not wrestle against flesh and blood, but against principalities, against powers, against the rulers of the darkness of this age, against spiritual hosts of wickedness in the heavenly places. Therefore take up the whole armour of God that you may be able to withstand in the evil day, and having done all, to stand.

Stand therefore, having girded your waist with truth, having put on the breastplate of righteousness, and having shod your feet with the preparation of the gospel of peace; above all, taking the shield of faith with which you will be able to quench all the fiery darts of the wicked one. And take the helmet of salvation, and the sword of the Spirit, which is the word of God".

To be successful in helping not only yourself, your loved ones, your friends, and even the cultist in which you are in dialogue with, it is absolutely necessary that you personally know Christ, or that you be in the company of a Born-again Christian who is filled with the Holy Spirit. A Born-again believer can exercise his authority in Jesus' Name, but a Spirit-filled believer can call on Spiritual weapons that he has access to! I believe that if you are not Born-again and Spirit-filled and you try to take on spiritual battles, then you will be just like a blindfold boxer in a ring – you won't even know who your opponent is and from what direction he is hitting you from? You won't even know where you opponent is to be able to hit him!

The Bible is not just a book of words on paper, it is the written Word of God and when it is used by true Christians it becomes ALIVE and POWERFUL, as the writer of Hebrews says:

"For the word of God is living and powerful, and sharper than any two-edged sword, piercing even to the division of soul and spirit, and of joints and marrow, and is a discerner of the thoughts and intents of the heart" (Hebrews 4:12).

Always Set Matters Straight With The Word of God

Still another reminder, you should make every effort to learn the Scriptures and be prepared when the time comes to prove the error of the particular cult that you are dealing with. Be able to back up from the Bible any 'reasoning' you may want to put forward. Be prepared to confidently share these Scriptures with the cultist directly from your own Bible. 2nd Timothy 3:16-17 says, *"All Scripture is given by inspiration of God, and is profitable for doctrine, for reproof, for correction, for instruction in righteousness, that the man of God may be complete, thoroughly equipped for ever good work."* – this is exactly what the Holy Spirit wants you to do!

When we know and share an appropriate portion of the Word with someone, it is then the Holy Spirit's job to take that word and minister it to the person you have shared it with. This is also why we stipulated that prayer must come both before and after your encounter with the one you are trying to help. Remember, the battle we are in is a spiritual one and can only be fought with spiritual weapons! If you feel the need for additional help and information, or literature to assist you to prepare such a presentation please visit our website[100], or your local Christian book store.

Some Facts About Satan

As a believer, you need have no fear of Satan, *"For God has not given us a spirit of fear, but of power and of love and of a sound mind* (2nd Timothy 1:7). Yes, you can overcome the harassment of Satan and his minions in the same way that Jesus did, by quoting the Word of God:

"Then Jesus was led up by the Spirit into the wilderness to be tempted by the devil. And when He had fasted forty days and forty nights,

---

[100] http://mandateministries.com.au

afterward He was hungry. Now when the tempter came to Him, he said, "If You are the Son of God, command that these stones become bread." But He answered and said, "It is written, 'Man shall not live by bread alone, but by every word that proceeds from the mouth of God.'"
Then the devil took Him up into the holy city, set Him on the pinnacle of the temple, and said to Him, "If You are the Son of God, throw Yourself down. For it is written: 'He shall give His angels charge over you,' and, 'In their hands they shall bear you up, Lest you dash your foot against a stone.'" Jesus said to him, "It is written again, 'You shall not tempt the LORD your God.'" Again, the devil took Him up on an exceedingly high mountain, and showed Him all the kingdoms of the world and their glory. And he said to Him, "All these things I will give You if You will fall down and worship me." Then Jesus said to him, "Away with you, Satan! For it is written, 'You shall worship the LORD your God, and Him only you shall serve.'" Then the devil left Him, and behold, angels came and ministered to Him." (Matthew 4:1-11; bolding added)

Jesus Christ once and for all time defeated and destroyed the works of the devil and his demons, on the Cross of Calvary. The Apostle John said, *"Little children, let no one deceive you. He who practices righteousness is righteous, just as He is righteous. He who sins is of the devil, for the devil has sinned from the beginning. For this purpose the Son of God was manifested, that He might destroy the works of the devil"* (1st John 3:7-8).

The devil and his demons have no power over true believers if they know how to stand their ground:

"We know that we are of God, and the whole world lies under the sway of the wicked one. And we know that the Son of God has come and has given us an understanding, that we may know Him who is true; and we are in Him who is true, in His Son Jesus Christ. This is the true God and eternal life" (1st John 5:19-20), and *"Beloved, do not believe every spirit, but test the spirits, whether they are of God; because many false prophets have gone out into the world. By this you know the Spirit of*

God: Every spirit that confesses that Jesus Christ has come in the flesh is of God, and every spirit that does not confess that Jesus Christ has come in the flesh is not of God. And this is the spirit of the Antichrist, which you have heard was coming, and is now already in the world. You are of God, little children, and have overcome them, because He who is in you is greater than he who is in the world. They are of the world. Therefore they speak as of the world, and the world hears them. We are of God. He who knows God hears us; he who is not of God does not hear us. By this we know the spirit of truth and the spirit of error" (1ˢᵗ John 4:1-5).

You can frustrate Satan's scheming by prayerfully binding him in the name of Jesus and nullifying all his efforts to steal and kill and destroy both you and your loved ones[101] by praying according to the principles outlined in the following Scriptures:

"...how can one enter a strong man's house and plunder his goods, unless he first binds the strong man? And then he will plunder his house" and *"No one can enter a strong man's house and plunder his goods, unless he first binds the strong man. And then he will plunder his house"* (Matthew 12:29 and Mark 3:27 respectively). What is described in the foregoing Scriptures is a spiritual act, which is known by all believing Christians as:

Spiritual Binding and Loosing

For example, if you know ahead of time that you will be entering into a discussion with a cultist, or sharing Scripture, prepare yourself by using your authority as a Christian and put Matthew 18:18-20 into action, which says,

---

[101] John 10:10, *"The thief does not come except to steal, and to kill, and to destroy. I have come that they may have life, and that they may have it more abundantly."*

"Assuredly, I say to you, whatever you bind on earth will be bound in heaven, and whatever you loose on earth will be loosed in heaven. "Again I say to you that if two of you agree on earth concerning anything that they ask, it will be done for them by My Father in heaven. For where two or three are gathered together in My name, I am there in the midst of them."

If you are new to all this, I very strongly recommended that you invite a believer to agree with you (not a doubter, but preferably a Born-again Spirit –filled Christian who is strong in their faith), and in Jesus' name, bind the spirit of deception which is keeping the cult member you are wanting to help blinded towards the truth (See 2nd Corinthians 4:4 and Acts 26:18). Then in prayer, 'loose' the cultist in Jesus' name, to hear the gospel of truth and ask that it will penetrate into his heart and mind and then decree him out of the kingdom of darkness and into the Kingdom of Light in Jesus' Holy Name!

Remember, that people in the cults are held by a 'spirit of deception', which keeps them in spiritual bondage. Your words of prayer will not have effect without Divine help, no matter how well prepared you are with information, logic, and even what seems to you like sound reasoning. Sadly, the writer has repeatedly shared this fact with many people over the years that one has to first deal with the 'spiritual' in order to set people not only 'physically' free from bondage, but also to be 'spiritually' free!

It grieves the writer that many over the years, including church leaders, have not taken this counsel seriously enough in order to win the 'spiritual war' for their loved ones, friends, and church members! Sadly, as is often the case, many years later, those who dismissed this advice, are still suffering from broken hearts, because their loved ones are still 'spiritually bound' by and belong to their cultic belief systems! Do not despair if results don't appear immediately. God's Word cannot go out and return without producing results. Isaiah 55:9-11 says:

"For as the heavens are higher than the earth, so are My ways higher than your ways, And My thoughts than your thoughts. For as the rain comes down, and the snow from heaven, And do not return there, But water the earth, And make it bring forth and bud, That it may give seed to the sower And bread to the eater, So shall My word be that goes forth from My mouth; It shall not return to Me void, But it shall accomplish what I please, And it shall prosper in the thing for which I sent it".

After you have prayed, be assured that the Word of God will begin working, under the influence of the Holy Spirit, in the cultist and with your continuing supportive prayers in time will convince him of his error. Never ever give up! Sometimes something significant has to happen in their cult group, or to them personally, or to others sadly that shocks and even hurts them, before they can start to doubt their pledged allegiance – you can even pray for division to break out amongst the leadership of their group that would be disconcerting to the members as a whole and unsettle them. It can also take time as they literally have to become uncomfortable in themselves with what they believe and practice – pray also that the Scriptures which they already know will be used by the Holy Spirit to unsettle them. If you don't pray for them, no one else will!

CHAPTER EIGHTEEN

How to Become a True Christian

Up until now, I've said much about being Born-again and how to fight 'spiritual wars'. I've also referred to the 'spirit realm', which for some of my readers may be very difficult to comprehend and understand, or even seem absurd? As a Born-again, Spirit-filled believer, my original intent in writing this book, was to help equip Christians to be able to fight back the onslaught of the cults – be they 'aberrant christian groups,' or 'other types' of cults.

However, I came to the realisation many years ago that we have been able to stand with many non-Christian people, who have come to us over the years, usually out of desperation, dearly wanting our help for a loved one, or friend, who has become involved with, or become a member of a cult.

This is why I felt it necessary to go more deeply into explaining the way in which a person can be introduced to Jesus

Christ, the one who said He was, "The way, and the truth and the life. No one comes to the Father, except through me"[102]

I believe that the evil that predominates in this world originally came about through Satan's rebellion which took place in Heaven[103]. He was of the highest order of angels. He was an Archangel who became filled with pride and became tempted to make himself to be as God. I realised that when that happened, that God the Father could have snuffed him out immediately, but he didn't – why? Because if he had done so, he would have become a God to fear and would no longer be a God of Love! The rest of creation were witnesses to what took place and they would have then known that if they 'stepped out of line' they would incur the same penalty and so be in fear of doing so!

I believe this is why the devil was in the Garden of Eden when God created mankind. The Bible tells us he was cast down to the earth and it became his dominion, or kingdom. 2nd Corinthians 4:4 says, *"The god of this age (world) has blinded the minds of unbelievers, so that they cannot see the light of the gospel that displays the glory of Christ, who is the image of God."* (Parenthesis mine). The 'god of this age' of course is Satan the Devil! The writer says that he, "…has blinded the minds of unbelievers" so that they cannot see the light of the Gospel! It also infers that he has deceived the unbelievers! I would ask the reader, are you a believer, or an unbeliever? If you are one or the other, then you should keep reading.

---

[102] John 14:6

[103] You can read about his rebellion in Ezekiel;28:1-19 which tells how and why he fell from Heaven to the Earth!

I believe that the reason that God created mankind was to demonstrate to the rest of His Creation, that the people he had introduced into 'satan's kingdom' would serve Him out of Love and not fear. It's also logical to me that is also why, when He created man, he made him to be a free moral agent, just like the angels, which gives him the ability to choose for himself as to whom he would serve – God the Father, who is a God of love, acceptance and forgiveness, or Satan, a wannabe god of rebellion and sin? If you would like to choose to be on God's side, then you need to become a Christian before it's too late as Satan's world and his followers are doomed for destruction and they will be judged for rejecting the invitation that was given through His Son, Jesus, when he said, *"Come to me, all you who are weary and burdened, and I will give you rest."* Please accept the invitation and read on for further instructions.

In his book *Born Again*[104], former US President Nixon's Watergate conspirator Charles (Chuck) Colson[105] describes his path to faith in conjunction with his criminal imprisonment and has played a significant role in solidifying the "Born again" identity as a cultural construct in the U.S.A.

He writes that his spiritual experience followed considerable struggle and hesitancy to have a "personal encounter

---

[104] Born Again, by Charles W. Colson, pp142-3, Chosen Books 2004.

In 1974 Charles W. Colson pleaded guilty to his involvement in the President Nixon Watergate Scandal. His related offenses revealed during the tumultuous investigation caused him to serve seven months in prison. In his search for meaning and purpose in the face of the scandal, Colson penned his book, 'Born Again.' This unforgettable memoir shows a man who was seeking fulfillment in striving for success and power. He actually found it, paradoxically, in national disgrace and in prison.[105]

with God." While this is Colson's testimony of his own encounter with Jesus Christ, it is not to imply that any certain pattern or model must be followed by others seeking a "Born again" Salvation relationship with Jesus. There is no formula for what to say nor certain experience to be anticipated or entered into. It is one's own way of professing faith in Christ as "Saviour", placing the whole of one's trust in Christ for eternal salvation...while I sat alone staring at the sea I love, words I had not been certain I could understand or say fell from my lips: *"Lord Jesus, I believe in You. I accept You. Please come into my life. I commit it to You."*

With these few words...came a sureness of mind that matched the depth of feeling in my heart. There came something more: strength and serenity, a wonderful new assurance about life, a fresh perception of myself in the world around me. In the process, I felt old fears, tensions and animosities training away. I was coming alive to things I'd never seen before; as if God was filling the barren void I'd known for so many months, filling it to its brim with a whole new kind of awareness.... I could not possibly in my wildest dreams have imagined what it would involve. How fortunate it is that God does not allow us to see into the future."

Chuck's experience is no different to that which is being experienced by thousands of others around the world daily. My own experience, when I was a teenager, was very similar. I was invited one night to visit with a Bible College student friend. He had been witnessing to me for several weeks and I was interested in what he was sharing with me. We sat in the lounge room of the house where he was staying. After talking together for some time, he asked me if I would like to accept the Lord Jesus Christ into my life and be Born-again? With my heart thumping, I nervously said "Yes"! He then invited me to kneel with him on the carpet. I did and he prayed a short prayer and then asked me to follow him in prayer, praying out loud, in a very similar manner to the one that Chuck Colson prayed. Because I sincerely wanted to become a Christian and be forgiven for what had become a very sinful life for me – God heard my prayer that night and I knew that He had cleansed me and made me new inside – I rose from the carpet knowing great joy, I was Born-again! I was not just a 'believer' in a Christ who once walked this earth, as many others do! My life changed dramatically from that point on. I had a desire to be in fellowship with other believers. I enjoyed being involved in church activities and for the first time ever, enjoyed reading my Old English King James Bible! By now you are probably wondering:

Why All The Emphasis On This Born-Again 'Thing'?

These days the term 'Born-again' seems to no longer be the exclusive use of Christians. In the media we frequently hear the term being used to describe a rejuvenated football team; or an athlete that's suffered loss after loss who now seems to be on a winning streak; even the release of a new model in a car series has been given the term! Therefore, it's important for us to look into the term's true meaning.

    In order for my reader to understand where I am coming from, I am going to have to use a lot of statements from the Bible. In most instances I will let them speak for themselves. As you are aware, I believe that the Bible is the inspired, written Word of God, and contains everything we need to know about God, His Son Jesus, the Holy Spirit and the Kingdom lifestyle he wants us to live. It even says of itself that, *"All Scripture is given by inspiration of God, and is profitable for doctrine* (teaching), *for reproof, for correction, for instruction in righteousness, that the man (or woman) of God may be complete, thoroughly equipped for every good work".*[106] (Parenthesis mine – I've quoted this Scripture a few times already!)

I've already made reference and placed an emphasis many times in this book for the need for one to be Born-again in order to understand 'spiritual matters' and to be equipped to 'fight spiritual battles'. But, you may still be wondering why I place such emphasis on it? It's worth explaining more deeply.

As we said in the previous Chapter, the Scriptural basis for the term 'Born-again' comes from the Bible Book of John[107] which we briefly mentioned and gave some insights into the reasons why you should consider how you can become a true Christian. I suggest you do, because as a Christian you will be in a better position to help, not only yourself, but your loved ones and others to avoid the deception and heresies and the cults.

Let's return and take another look at the record of the secretive discussion that took place when Nicodemus, who we now know was a very religious and pious man, who came seeking answers for his dilemma and to speak with Jesus at night[108]. He was one of the top Jewish leaders of his day in the time of Christ. I believe it would be appropriate to read the full account of their conversation once more and I will then comment on it further:

"There was a man of the Pharisees named Nicodemus, a ruler of the

---

[106] 2 Timothy 3:16-17

[107] Chapter 3:1-14

[108] Just like Nicodemus, while I was looking for answers during the Vietnam War years, I would make appointments at night to see various ministers seeking their help for my dilemma. I thought no one could see me under the cover of darkness!

Jews.[109] *This man came to Jesus by night and said to Him, "Rabbi, we know that You are a teacher come from God; for no one can do these signs that You do unless God is with him. "Jesus answered and said to him, "Most assuredly, I say to you, <u>unless one is born again, he cannot see the kingdom of God</u>." Nicodemus said to Him, "How can a man be born when he is old? Can he enter a second time into his mother's womb and be born?" Jesus answered, "Most assuredly, I say to you, <u>unless one is born of water and the Spirit, he cannot enter the kingdom of God</u>. That which is born of the flesh is flesh, and that which is born of the Spirit is spirit. Do not marvel that I said to you, 'You must be born again.' The wind blows where it wishes, and you hear the sound of it, but cannot tell where it comes from and where it goes. So is everyone who is born of the Spirit. "Nicodemus answered and said to Him, "How can these things be?" Jesus answered and said to him, "Are you the teacher of Israel, and do not know these things? Most assuredly, I say to you, We speak what We know and testify what We have seen, and you do not receive Our witness. <u>If I have told you earthly things and you do not believe, how will you believe if I tell you heavenly things?</u> No one has ascended to heaven but He who came down from heaven, that is, the Son of Man who is in heaven. And as Moses lifted up the serpent in the wilderness, even so must the Son of Man be lifted up..."*

In the foregoing account of Jesus's discussion, which is probably one of the most important one's in the New Testament regarding

---

[109] Nicodemus was a member of the Sanhedrin which was the name given in the Mishna* to the council of seventy-one Jewish sages who constituted the supreme court and legislative body in Judea during the Roman period. *An authoritative collection of explanations and/or interpretations of a religious text, embodying the oral tradition of Jewish law and forming the first part of the Talmud. The Talmud is the body of Jewish civil and ceremonial law and legend, of which there are two versions, the Babylonian Talmud and the Jerusalem Talmud.

how one may obtain Salvation. Sadly what we are going to address will be of little or of no importance to many. It is overlooked, even ignored, by many people in the Church today, sadly including many church leaders! Over many years, I have asked hundreds of people seeking our guidance and help, the question, "Are you a Christian?" Many have replied, some thoughtfully some not, by saying many different things like some of the following statements:

"I think I have to be, I was born into a Christian family?"; "I hope that I am, I always try and do good to others?";"I struggle with that but I try to do the best that I know how."; "My Aunty was a Nun."; "Well, I go to church almost every Sunday, when I can"; "Ah…um…ah…well to be honest, I'm not really sure that I am"; "I was Confirmed in the church when I was a youngster; "My Grandfather was a minister."; "I got baptised in water years ago because my friend asked me to do it with her"; "I used to be an Altar Boy." ;"Well, I've always been in church. My mother used to send me to Sunday School when I was young."; I must be a Christian because I play Christian music CD's in my car when I go shopping."; "I took my first communion when I was 7 years-old"

Sadly, all of the foregoing responses and there are many others like them, have absolutely nothing to do with helping someone to find Salvation and become a true Christian! The ancient Bible character Job makes the point that it is an individual's responsibility to make the decision to become a Christian. He says, *"Now acquaint yourself with Him, and be at peace; Thereby good will come to you".*[110] There is only one way for us to be able to be at peace and have good come to us in this life and that is

---

[110] Job 22:21

for us to acquaint ourselves with God. How do we do that you may be asking? By taking heed of the provision of His written Word, the Bible, and taking and applying the advice it gives us when it comes to knowing God. The Bible clearly teaches that God the Father is knowable and even Jesus said that he came to earth to reveal the Father to us! *"If you had known Me, you would have known My Father also; and from now on you know Him and have seen Him."*[111] So the key to getting acquainted with God is to get to know the only true Saviour, His Son, Jesus Christ!

However, for many non-Christians that statement poses a problem? Jesus is repeatedly referred to in the Scriptures as being mankind's Saviour. Please note what Peter said about getting to know God, *"To those who have obtained like precious faith with us by the righteousness of our God and Saviour Jesus Christ."*[112] So, Jesus is the Saviour, but what do we need to be Saved from? The Apostle Paul tells us, in no uncertain terms, very clearly what the answer to that question is? He said in Ephesians 2:1-2, *"And you He made alive, who were dead in trespasses*[113] *and sins, in which you once walked according to the course of this world, according to the prince of the power of the air, the spirit who now works in the sons of disobedience..."*

Therefore, I think it is very clear that unless we are Born-again' (or, experience what is called a *'new birth'* -which means having our spirits spiritually regenerated by the Holy Spirit – or being

---

[111] Jesus said, "If you had known Me, you would have known My Father also; and from now on you know Him and have seen Him." John 14:7

[112] 2nd Peter 1:1

[113] Throughout the Bible, "trespass" is used to describe either the violation of the rights of other people, or disobedience to God.

made alive unto God) we are simply dead in our 'trespasses and sins'!

To reinforce the fact that we are 'sinners' in need of a Saviour, Paul continues in v3, *"...among whom also we all once conducted ourselves in the lusts of our flesh, fulfilling the desires of the flesh and of the mind, and were by nature children of wrath, just as the others"*. Then, in Psalm 51:5 King David tells us exactly how mankind becomes 'sinful' by saying, *"Behold, I was brought forth in iniquity[114] and in sin my mother conceived me."* This does not mean what many think, it is implying that from the moment Adam and Eve rebelled and sinned against God, that every child she and other women have conceived since then is born into a sinful world! Therefore, apart from the new birth, and having our spirit made alive unto God, we are generally by nature children of wrath, or angry and not at all at peace.

The Apostle John puts it this way, *"And this is the condemnation, that the light has come into the world, and men loved darkness rather than light, because their deeds were evil. For everyone practicing evil hates the light and does not come to the light, lest his deeds should be exposed. But he who does the truth comes to the light, that his deeds may be clearly seen, that they have been done in God."*[115] Therefore, apart from receiving the new birth, mankind loves darkness and hates light![116]

Note what the following Scriptures have to say about our

---

[114] Here 'iniquity' means 'a lack of justice or righteousness' which, as said previously came about when the first man, Adam, chose to not obey God and was cast out of the Garden of Eden as a result. Jesus came to redeem the life that Adam lost!

[115] John 3:19-20

[116] Most crimes and unspeakable acts are committed at night!

spiritual condition, *"I will give you a new heart and put a new spirit within you; I will take the <u>heart of stone</u> out of your flesh and give you a heart of flesh."* Ezekiel 36:26,

"...having their understanding darkened, being alienated from the life of God, because of the ignorance that is in them, because of <u>the blindness of their heart</u>..." Ephesians 4:18

"For the wrath of God is revealed from heaven against all ungodliness and unrighteousness of men, who <u>suppress the truth in unrighteousness...</u>" Romans 1:18

As a result of our inherited sinful state how and what can we do to change things for the better you may be thinking? Paul describes the state we are in when he says, *"...the carnal mind is enmity against God; for it is not subject to the law of God, nor indeed can be. So then, those who are in the flesh cannot please God".* Romans 8:7-8 Therefore, apart from the receiving the new birth, our hearts are hard like stone; our minds are blind; and we suppress the truth.

How then can we do what Job counselled us to do about becoming acquainted with God? For the answer, let's go back to our discussion with Jesus and Nicodemus: *"Jesus answered, "Most assuredly, I say to you, <u>unless one is born of water and the Spirit, he cannot enter the kingdom of God."</u>* John 3:5 What Jesus is saying here, clearly shows us that apart from receiving the <u>new birth</u>, we are unable to submit to God, or please Him, and we cannot enter into his Kingdom for all Eternity!

In the foregoing Scripture, note the statement *unless one is born of water and the Spirit.* Years ago, I used to think, as many do, that to be *born of water* referred to water baptism, but I no longer think that! What I now believe is that Jesus is referring to one of the last things that happens before we are born in to this world – and that is, our mother's water has to break! (I'll say more on this shortly). I believe that what Jesus is referring to here is that you have to be born naturally into this world before you can accept the invitation to be *born of the Spirit* and become totally Born-again!

This is why I also believe, as we will see, that those in the 'spirit realm' that belong to Satan's kingdom, who were not born naturally into this world, want to try to 'possess' (or 'inhabit') a human body in attempt to avoid the sad future that they know is in store for them – that is to be thrown into the Lake of Fire! [117]

"...you should no longer walk as the rest of the Gentiles walk, in the futility of their mind, having their understanding darkened, being alienated from the life of God, because of the ignorance that is in them, because of the blindness of their heart..." Ephesians 4:17b-18

"But the natural man does not receive the things of the Spirit of God, for they are foolishness to him; nor can he know them, because they are spiritually discerned." 1st Corinthians 2:14 Hopefully, one can now see that apart from receiving the <u>new birth</u>, we are unable to accept the truth of the Gospel, or receive the Good News that Jesus came to save us from our sins. The Apostle John wrote the following: *"No one can come to Me unless the Father who sent Me draws him; and I*

---

[117] The Lake of Fire was created for the devil and his angels. The demonic realm therefore has no redeemer. Jesus did not bear their sins in His body. He bore OUR sins in his body (1 Pet 2:24 says , *"who Himself bore our sins in His own body on the tree, that we, having died to sins, might live for righteousness—by whose stripes you were healed."*). Since the devil and his angels do NOT have a sin-bearer, they remain in their sins. Their punishment is eternal. Since there will be sinful and unrepentant people thrown into that SAME Lake of Fire, their punishment will also be eternal.

will raise him up at the last day..." And He said, *"Therefore I have said to you that no one can come to Me unless it has been granted to him by My Father."* John 6:44, 65. Then Paul wrote, *"Therefore I make known to you that no one speaking by the Spirit of God calls Jesus accursed, and no one can say that Jesus is Lord except by the Holy Spirit."* 1st Corinthians 12:3. Apart from receiving the <u>new birth</u>, we are unable to come to Christ and embrace Him as Lord of our lives!

The Garden of Eden

Let's go back to the beginning. In Genesis 2:15-17 it states, *"Then the LORD God took the man and put him in the Garden of Eden to tend and keep it. And the LORD God commanded the man, saying, "Of every tree of the garden you may freely eat; but of the tree of the knowledge of good and evil you shall not eat, for in the day that you eat of it you shall surely die."* The word 'die' is translated from the Hebrew word *mûth* and means 'to die (literally or figuratively); causatively to kill; to put to death, to destroy; or cause to die suddenly...'!

Almost everyone who knows the Bible account is aware that Adam and Eve disobeyed God's instruction and they ate the fruit! So, if God's word is truth and it's impossible for Him to lie, then when they disobeyed, something had to die just as he said? So what was it that died? I believe that it was their 'spiritual connection', or relationship with God, their Creator and Father! After both Adam and Eve sinned they were still body, soul and spirit in their makeup, but they were now 'dead spiritually' towards their Creator! And that's where all of mankind's problems began!

This is the reason why man, without God in his life always desires to worship someone, or something! He still has a 'spirit' that longs to do what it was created for, to worship and serve

God!~It may be a stone idol he builds; it can be a tree; or a Crucifix (Jesus is not still on the Cross – He was taken from the Cross and laid in a tomb. However, the Good News, or Gospel, is that He has risen from the dead!); it could be amassing material possessions; it could be an animal; for many it is money, and so the list goes on. Everyone has a need to be satisfied spiritually! The problem for us is that that we try to fill our 'spiritual vacuum' with all the wrong things. This is also why people join cults!

Titus 3:4-7 shows us the way to get to know God personally, or to get acquainted with him. Paul writes, *"...when the kindness and the love of God our Saviour toward man appeared, not by works of righteousness which we have done, but according to His mercy He saved us, through the washing of regeneration* and renewing of the Holy Spirit, whom He poured out on us abundantly through Jesus Christ our Saviour, that having been justified by His grace we should become heirs according to the hope of eternal life."* *The Greek word used here is: *paliggenesia* which literally means 'spiritual rebirth, or spiritual renovation' for the human spirit!

Writer Michael Bradley says, "First, regeneration is being directly tied to us getting saved in the Lord. The words *"but according to His mercy He saved us, through the washing of regeneration and renewing of the Holy Spirit"* are definitely telling us that we are saved by God's grace and mercy and that when He does save us – He is saving us "through" the regeneration of our spirit by the Holy Spirit. Second, this regeneration is done directly by the Holy Spirit Himself. The words "regeneration and renewing of the Holy Spirit" are telling us that this regeneration is being done directly by the Holy Spirit Himself." From the Scriptures we have read, I believe we now know that mankind lives under 'a curse' because of Adam's sin of disobedience towards God and wanting to be 'like

God'. Romans 3:23 says, *"for all have sinned and fall short of the glory of God."*

This is because we are born naturally as physical beings – but of our spirit it can be said that it is 'still-born' spiritually towards God and true spiritual things.[118] This is the reason why the majority of mankind has had difficulty understanding the difference between what is true and false spirituality! This line of reasoning also begs the question, "If our 'spirit' needs to be regenerated, in order to become 'alive' to the things of God – what is it that we must we do?"

To answer, let's go back to Jesus and Nicodemus again and see how Jesus responded to the first question that he was asked? He replied, *"...I say to you, unless one is <u>born again</u>[119], **he cannot <u>see</u> the Kingdom of God</u>"*Please note that he is saying that unless one is Born-again, he can't even **see** the Kingdom of God! Note His response to the second questions in v5, *"Jesus answered, "...unless one is born of water and the Spirit, **he cannot <u>enter</u> the kingdom of God."*** That obviously means what is says - if you are not Born-again you can't even see or enter the Kingdom of God?

In the preceding Scripture, I believe that where Jesus uses the term, 'born of water' if we look to the Greek again, we find that he is referring to just 'water'. The term is derived from a root word which means 'to rain, or shower'! This fact caused a question to arise for me (the answer to which I've already partly alluded to), how can it have anything to do with water baptism by

---

[118] John 4:24 says, "God is Spirit, and those who worship Him must worship in spirit and truth."

[119] In John Chapter 3 the words 'born again' in Greek mean: *from above, again, anew*

immersion[120] as many would have us believe? Question? Is it possible for one immerse oneself in a downpour of rain, or under a shower? The answer of course is "No"! One can only be 'immersed' in a body of water![121]

As I mentioned before, in Verse 5, I believe that where it says 'born of water' is simply referring to the natural physical birth of a child into this world. When a pregnant mother comes to full term her waters will break, or have to be broken, before the birth of her child. My understanding here is that Jesus is implying that only those who are born naturally into this earth can see and enter the Kingdom of God, but only if they are Born-again. That naturally rules out any other spirit being, like an angel or a demon – for whom there is no provision for them to be 'born-again' – thus ruling them out of participating in God's plan for mankind to be with him Eternally! I often wonder if the reason demons want to possess a person's body is because they know that one has to be in a physical earthly body first before they can get back into Heaven?

Now let us look at the Greek word for 'Spirit', which is *Pneuma*. When spelt with a capital 'P' it refers to the Holy Spirit, the third person of the Trinity. Without the capital 'P' it refers to 'a current of air', or a 'breath'; which comes from a root word denoting 'forcible respiration' which for me it implies that when

---

[120] The Greek word for 'baptise' is *baptízō* – properly, meaning to 'submerge'; hence, baptise, is to immerse (literally, to "dip under"). 907 (baptízō) implies submersion ("immersion"), in contrast to 472 /antéxomai (to "sprinkle"). (Strong's)

[121] For a Scriptural example of how one comes to know Jesus as their Saviour and is baptised in water, please read the account of Phillip and the Ethiopian in Acts *:26-39

He is invited the Holy Spirit brings into a person 'new life'. When a person accepts Christ as their personal Lord and Saviour and they are Born-again, they can then say, *"I have been crucified with Christ; it is no longer I who live, but Christ lives in me; and the life which I now live in the flesh I live by faith in the Son of God, who loved me and gave Himself for me."*

The Term 'born-again' is of Jewish Origin

To the Jews the term 'born again' referred to a non-Jew who had undergone a formal conversion to Judaism. The Talmud (the Jewish oral law) states, "When he comes up after his immersion, he is deemed an Israelite in all respects." (Yevamot 47b) Rabbi Yose says in the Talmud, "One who has become a proselyte is <u>like a child newly born</u>." (Yevamot 48b) This is why a person who is not of Jewish descent, when he converts to Judaism, after a lengthy period of study and testing he, or she, is then immersed in the waters of the *Mikvah* (pool[122]). On exiting the water and climbing up the steps, the convert is regarded as actualising the transition they have made from their old identity to his or her new identity as a member of the Jewish faith.

It has been likened to a 'rebirth', so much so, that the convert is given a new name – which will be a Jewish name! So when Jesus told Nicodemus that unless he was born again, he could not see, nor could he enter the Kingdom of God, he was able to understand something of what the term actually meant. Because of his longevity and years of study of the Hebrew Scriptures coupled with his knowledge of Jewish traditions, the

---

[122] The Mikvah was so important to the Jewish people that tradition held that it had to be built first before they could build a synagogue.

Bible account tells us that Nicodemus went on to become a believer and follower of Jesus as a Born-again Christian!

The Bible test you must pass to be a true Christian

When there is some doubt as to whether a person is a genuine Christian or not, there is a Biblical test that can be put to them. If they fail the test then they cannot be accepted as holding to the true Faith! The Apostle Paul tells us exactly what that test is, when he writes, *"Examine yourselves as to whether you are in the faith. Test yourselves. Do you not know yourselves that **Jesus Christ is in you?**[123]— unless indeed you are <u>disqualified</u> (or, failed the test!)."*[124] Therefore, if the person cannot positively tell you that Jesus Christ is 'in' him and tell you when and what he did to have him come 'in', then they have failed the test! (Underlining mine)

From my experience, when you begin to counsel with someone you do not know, it is the most important and probably should be the very first question you should ask, to understand where they are spiritually! Let me ask my reader, "Can you honestly say that, Jesus Christ is in you?" Please turn to Appendices 3 and 4 for two illustrations as to how the English word *'in'* and the Greek word *'en' are* used grammatically in both languages? This will help to grasp why the meaning and context of the word *'in'* that Paul uses here, in his letter to the Corinthians, is so extremely important to ask a person who claims to be a

---

[123] Turning to the Greek again. The word 'in' used here is 'en' which is a primary preposition meaning to "remain within". The phrase, "Jesus Christ is in you" is from root words denoting "a fixed position in place, time or state"!

[124] 2nd Corinthians 13:5

Christian and has the audacity to try and tell you that you are in the wrong church!

If you try and counsel a person using Christian principles from the Bible and he or she is not Born-again, then you can counsel with them until the 'cows-come-home' and you will probably achieve exactly nothing! If a person is not sure that he is Born-again and gives you a wrong answer when you ask the question, then he is not a new creation in Christ! Your first priority in counselling, or reasoning with anyone who does not know the Born-again experience, you should try to get them to recognise that they are a sinner and in need of a Saviour before you proceed further!

Christian Psychology?

Many well-meaning Christians, devoid of spiritual insight, have allowed something that has been labelled as 'Christian Psychology' (which I personally call 'Psycho Babble'), to slowly infiltrate the church's counselling role! I have probably now thrown yet 'another cat among the pigeons' by mentioning the term, "Christian Psychology" in a negative way? Why what's wrong with that, you may be thinking? In the early part of this writing, I stressed the need to examine the roots of various dangerous religious groups and their teachings. Well, many years ago, because of circumstances, I took my own advice and dug down into the roots of psychiatry and psychology. What I found was not 'pretty' and as a result, like Jay Adams[125] I really believe that we

---

[125] Jay Adams, Professor of Practical Theology, Westminster Theological Seminary and a well-known Biblical counsellor and author of over 100 books.

have everything we need in Scripture to effectively counsel the cultist, the occultist, or anyone else's problems for that matter!

A number of people who were having problems caused by the cults, who eventually came to us for help, told us that they were referred by their minister, or pastor, to a "Professional Counsellor" to receive the help that they thought they could not offer! One 'counsellor' told me that the main reason that people join cults is, "They have an addictive personality because they are predisposed to addictions"! For me that was just a load of Codswallop!

It was author's Dave Hunt (who, with his wife Ruth, stayed with us in Sydney years ago when on holiday from the US.) and his ministry partner T.A. McMahon[126] who were both responsible for causing me to investigate the roots of psychiatry and psychology for myself. What inspired me to do so was that I had read an article in one of their publications, which said, "The Freudian/Jungian myths of psychic determinism and the unconscious have been so universally accepted that these unfounded assumptions now exert a major influence upon Christian thinking throughout the church...As a major vehicle of the seduction that unites most of its elements, psychology is the Trojan horse par excellence that has slipped past every barrier."[127]

He continually promoted and counselled the truth of Scripture rather than the psychological opinions of men.

[126] Christian Apologists Dave Hunt and T.A. McMahon, joined forces to create 'The Berean Call', under the direction of Dave Hunt for the purpose of encouraging spiritual discernment among those who regarded themselves not just as "evangelicals" but as biblical Christians. The website: http://www.thebereancall.org/

[127] *The Seduction of Christianity.* (Eugene: Harvest House, 1985), p189

In all my years of counselling victims of cultic deception and their false teachings and practices, including many war veterans from WWII, Korea and the Vietnam Wars, I have yet to meet anyone who has been successfully counselled in the area of spiritual matters relating to their emotional and behavioural disorders by a psychiatrist or psychologist that had a beneficial and lasting effect? Where there are indications of the works of demonic deception and influence, you cannot medicate or use worldly theories, manmade techniques and other methods to get rid of them!

The most eye-opening book that I read in my research was one written by Martin and Deidre Bobgan.[128] On page 5 under the heading, What About "Christian Psychology"? This is what they wrote, "Well-meaning psychologists who profess Christianity have merely borrowed the theories and techniques from secular psychology. They dispense what they believe to be the perfect blend of psychology and Christianity. Nevertheless, the psychology they use is the same as that used by non-Christian psychologists and psychiatrists. They use the theories and techniques devised by such men as Freud, Jung, Rogers, Janov, Ellis, Adler, Berne, Fromm, Maslow, and others, none of whom embraced Christianity or developed a psychological system from the Word of God"!

The United States Christian Association for Psychological Studies (CAPS) is a made up of a group of psychologists and

---

[128] *Psycho Heresy – The Psychological Seduction of Christianity*, 1987 by EastGate Publishers, Santa Barbara, California, USA

psychological counsellors who are all professing Christians. At one of their meetings the following was recorded as being said:

"We are often asked are we "Christian Psychologists" and (we) find it difficult to answer since we don't know what the question implies. We are Christians who are psychologists but at the present time there is no acceptable Christian psychology that is markedly different from non-Christian psychology. It is difficult to imply that we function in a manner that is fundamentally distinct from our non-Christian colleagues…as yet there is not an acceptable theory, mode of research or treatment methodology that is distinctly Christian."[129] They have no idea!

You can see why I have very little confidence, in fact none at all, when it comes to people in the church counselling others who hold to worldly techniques and theories. Far better for us as Christian people who counsel to use the Word of God (the Bible) and be led by the Holy Spirit and use the Gifts of the Holy Spirit that he supplies and empowers us with. The Holy Spirit can give us words of wisdom, words of knowledge, words of faith, healings, miraculous powers, prophecy (insight), distinguishing of spirits and so on.[130] These are more than sufficient to be able to be more than competent to counsel! Timothy was told by the Apostle Paul that: *"All Scripture is given by inspiration of God, and is profitable for doctrine, for reproof, for correction, for instruction in righteousness, that the man of God may be complete, thoroughly*

---

[129] Sutherland, P. and Poelstra, P. "Aspects of Integration". Paper presented at the meeting of the Western Association of Christians for Psychological Studies, Santa Barbara, CA, June 1976

[130] 1st Corinthians 12:1-11

equipped for every good work."[131] I believe that Scriptural counselling is a very 'good work'![132]

Let's now go back to the person you have established is not a Born-again Believer. After explaining to them some of the information we have suggested, and the need to be Saved, if the person is willing, you could then ask to pray with them and lead them in a prayer, perhaps similar to the one Charles Colson and I prayed, or perhaps something like the sample prayer on Page 154?

---

[131] 2nd Timothy 3:16-17
[132] For futher insight go to: http://www.gotquestions.org/nouthetic-counseling.html

THE SIMPLE GOSPEL IN 10 POINTS

If children can understand this, why is it that certain people want to make it much more complicated and won't accept this as it is?

1. Everybody has sinned

2. God hates sin

3. Sin must be punished

4. Jesus took the punishment instead of us on the cross

5. Admit you have been naughty

6. Believe that Jesus took your punishment

7. Say sorry to God

8. Ask God to be in charge of your life

9. Be baptised in water

10. Receive the Holy Spirit

    (Please note the order in the above!)

CHAPTER NINETEEN

Know Your Position in Christ

Please note where the writer of Ephesians, the Apostle Paul, tells us our spiritual blessings come from and that he speaks in the present tense, *"Blessed be the God and Father of our Lord Jesus Christ, who has blessed us with every spiritual blessing in the heavenly places in Christ"* (1:3). He continues in verses 17-21:

"... that the God of our Lord Jesus Christ, the Father of glory, may give to you the spirit of wisdom and revelation in the knowledge of Him, the eyes of your understanding being enlightened; that you may know what is the hope of His calling, what are the riches of the glory of His inheritance in the saints, and what is the exceeding greatness of His power toward us who believe, according to the working of His mighty power which He worked in Christ when He raised Him from the dead and <u>seated Him at His right hand in the heavenly places, far above all principality and power and might and dominion, and every name that is named, not only in this age but also in that which is to come.</u>"

Please note where it says Christ was enthroned when He returned to Heaven – at the right hand of God in *heavenly places*, far above all principality and power and might and dominion. Now let's look at what Scripture says happens to us when we are Born-again? In 2:5-6 it says, *"...even when we were dead in trespasses, made us alive together with Christ (by grace you have been saved), and <u>raised us up together, and made us sit together in the heavenly places in Christ Jesus</u>..."*

The moment a person is Born-again, he is immediately enthroned, or seated, with Christ! Colossians 1:13 confirms this fact when it says. *"He has delivered us from the power of darkness and conveyed us into the kingdom of the Son of His love..."* We've been 'conveyed into another kingdom! The word 'power' used here can also be translated as 'territory, colony, or kingdom'. So the word 'convey' implies we've been taken spiritually from one kingdom to another! What actually happened was that we have been made 'Citizens of Heaven' just as the Scripture says. If we are 'seated with Christ' we have enrolled in training to be the Kings and Priests that it says we will be in Revelation 1:6, *"...and has made us kings and priests to His God and Father, to Him be glory and dominion forever and ever."*

What an incredible result! Chapter 5:10 tells us, *"...And have made us kings and priests to our God; and we shall reign on the earth."* Paul, knowing the Scriptures, reinforces this in Romans 5:17 where he says that in this life, we Christians should be doing what kings do, and that it to 'Reign', for he states, *"For if by the one man's (Adam) offense death reigned through the one, much more those who receive abundance of grace and of the gift of righteousness will <u>reign in life</u> through the One, Jesus Christ."*[133] That definitely means us, now and in this life!   (Parenthesis and underlining added)

Therefore, our goal and role in this life as Christians should be that of Kings and Priests! The Scripture says we are, so

---

[133] For further references as to who we are in this life, go to: John 14:12-13; Romans 8:14, 16, 31 & 37; Philippians 4:13

we are tasked with being people who 'Reign in this life'! We have to learn and be trained in how to exercise our delegated authority from Christ. His authority comes from a higher source than the one who Paul in Ephesians 2:2 said when he was referring to the kingdom that we are grounded in before we become Born-again! He says, *"...in which you once walked according to the course of this world, according to the prince of the power of the air, the spirit who now works in the sons of disobedience..."* The 'Prince' mentioned here is not Jesus! He is none other than the devil, Satan himself! The word 'air' in this passage is the Greek word *'kosmos'*[134] of which we will say more to say shortly.

All of the foregoing is why we need to fully understand that when we became a Citizen of Heaven that we are now living in this world as purely as 'Ambassadors for Christ'. Although we live on earth, we are no longer of this dominion, or world *(kosmos)*.

With this in mind it makes it easy to understand what Paul meant when he said, *"If then you were raised with Christ, seek those things which are above, where Christ is, sitting at the right hand of God. Set your mind on things above, not on things on the earth. For <u>you died, and your life is hidden with Christ in God</u>. When Christ who is our life appears, then you also will appear with Him in glory."* Colossians 3:1-4 (Underlining mine)

Let us now spend some time and see what we can learn from Scripture and what we need to recognise about our new position in the Christ, or the Universe, in order for us to be

---

[134] The word cosmonaut derives from the Greek *"kosmos"*

complete and equipped and competent for every good work as Paul encouraged Timothy he should be doing?[135]

Hebrew Understanding of the Heavens

In Scripture, the phrase, "heaven and earth" is used many times to define the whole universe.[136] According to the Hebrew notion, or understanding, there were three (3) heavens. The following Bible references are all, but one, taken from the Hebrew, or Jewish Scriptures.

(1) The First Heaven was called by the Hebrews 'the firmament', meaning 'Sky' [137]) which they conceived as a solid dome. Bible History Online says, "... The firmament was created by God on the second day to separate the "waters from the waters" (Genesis 1:6-7)[138]. Another use of the word "heaven" in the Bible is to refer to the ceiling or canopy above the earth. Heaven in this sense is referred to as being, Sky (see Genesis 1:8)".[139]

(2) The Second Heaven for the Hebrews was called the 'Starry Heavens' which was what they could see at night. In ancient Bible times they were thought to be living creatures[140]. Many ancient religions held similar beliefs. For example, the Assyrians, kinsmen of the Hebrews, likewise conceived of the

---

[135] 2nd Timothy 3:16-17

[136] Gen 1:1; Jer 23:24; Acts 17:24

[137] "Firmament". Catholic Encyclopedia. New York: Robert Appleton Company. 1913

[138] The Bible speaks of the 'waters above' (windows of Heaven) and the 'waters below" (fountains of the deep).

[139] http://www.bible-history.com/faussets/F/Firmament/

[140] http://www.jewishencyclopedia.com/articles/2052-astronomy

stars as being soldiers serving the god of heaven, Anu, and probably also the somewhat similar god Ninib. The stars are again referred to in Deuteronomy 17:3; Jeremiah 8:2 and in then in Matthew 24:29 where it speaks of the second coming of Jesus when it says, "the stars will fall from heaven".

(3) The Third Heaven for the Hebrew people, is translated either as "the heaven of the heavens" or "the third heaven" in English from Deuteronomy 10:14; 1 Kings 8:27; Psalm 115:16, 148:4.

As an aside, the Hebrew word 'galgal'[141] is from where the word *galaxy* comes which can be translated as, wheel, wheels, whirlwind, whirling dust, or 'heaven a rolling thing'!

The Christian Understanding of the Heavens

Just as there are different meanings in Hebrew for the 'heavens, the same occurs in *Koine Greek,* the language used in the Christian Greek Scriptures. There are five (5) different Greek words that translate into English as heaven, heavenly places, and mid-heaven. It is most important for a Christian to get to know the difference as it will effect his view of this world and his position in Christ! Those five words are (See Chart at end of the Chapter):

1. ***KOSMOS*** - Which translates as 'world', or the earth, and 'air' or, the atmosphere around it. It is the word that is used in Ephesians 2:2 where it speaks of Satan as being, "the prince of the power of the air (or, *kosmos)*"

---

[141] Strongs *1534*

2. ***OURANOS*** – Which translates as 'stars' and 'galaxies'. It is derived from the root word, *'ornumi'* which means, 'to lift, or 'to heave' the latter from which we get the word 'heavens'. In Hebrews 4:14[142] it is the *'Ouranos'* which Jesus passed through when he ascended on high.

3. ***MEZOURANEMA*** – This word is where we get our word 'mezanine'. It means, 'a place between, or a boundary between two places', e.g., a 'mezzanine floor' in a building is a floor in between two floors. In Revelation 8:13 John says, *"...I looked, and I heard an angel flying through the midst of heaven (mezouranema)..."*

4. ***EPOURANIOUS*** – This is the most important one for Christians to know about as this is the Heaven where and over what Christ sits! Ephesians 1:20 says, *"...He worked in Christ when He raised Him from the dead and seated Him at His right hand in the heavenly places (epouranious) far above all principality and power and might and dominion, and every name that is named, not only in this age but also in that which is to come."*

Therefore, now we know exactly where Christ is seated, that makes this next Scripture quote from Ephesians 2:4-6 extremely important for us to take on board, *"God, who is rich in mercy, because of His great love with which He loved us, even when we were dead in trespasses, made us alive together with Christ (by grace you have been saved), and raised us up together, and made us sit together in the heavenly places (<u>epouranious</u>) in Christ Jesus..."* This instructs us that as Christians we are no longer people of this world *(kosmos)* at the very moment we were Born-again, we were spiritually

---

[142] "Seeing then that we have a great High Priest who has passed through the heavens *(ouranos)*, Jesus the Son of God, let us hold fast our confession."

translated out of the *kosmos* and into the *epouanious,* which is the Third Heaven!

The *epouranious* is the same place that Paul said he was caught up to when he said of himself, *"I know a man in Christ who fourteen years ago—whether in the body I do not know, or whether out of the body I do not know, God knows—such a one was caught up to the third heaven (epouranious)."*

5. **OURANOTHEN** – This is the 'heaven' that really allowed all of the foregoing Greek words, once I understood them, to fall into place for me! The Apostle Paul in recounting his testimony of how he became a Christian, when standing before King Agrippa, he said, *"...at midday, O king, along the road I saw a light from <u>heaven</u>, brighter than the sun, shining around me and those who journeyed with me."* The word *heaven* used here is not one of the previous four words! This fifth word literally means, "the uncreated sphere of God's dwelling place"! The word comes from a root word meaning, 'God's abode' or 'the Heaven where God lives! This answered for me the question about where was God before the universe was created? Obviously, there is much more for us to learn?

The foregoing also answered a lot of other questions for me when I was learning the truth and discarding all the wrong teachings that I had taken on board in my time with the Jehovah's Witnesses. It was while learning things like the foregoing that I began to understand why Paul referred to us as being, "ambassadors for Christ, God making his appeal through us."[143]

---

[143] 2 Corinthians 5:20

We have been given a ministry of reconciliation and the message of reconciling the world to God![144]

The Heaven's Chart

I designed the chart below back in the mid-1980's and it has been used frequently over the years to illustrate where we are seated with Christ in the *Epouranious*. It also reveals why we have power and authority over the 'spirits of darkness', who are confined to the *Kosmos!*, or the Earth

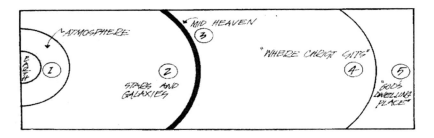

Therefore, being seated with Christ, we are able to overcome all the devious strategies of the Evil One and function as we are called to be, Ambassadors for Christ! Everywhere we go on this earth, we are off-limits to the Kingdom of Darkness. Because Satan's dominion is anchored in the *kosmos* – in fact one could say that as ambassadors representing another kingdom that we 'have diplomatic immunity' from the wiles and deceptions of the Devil's kingdom!

---

[144] Ibid Verses 18-21

CHAPTER TWENTY

Summary and Conclusions

Now that we have come this far, what should we conclude about the many cultic groups that grow like noxious weeds in our society today? Are we going to be 'politically correct' as society wants us to be and just stand by and do nothing? Or, as Christians are we going to stand against them on the authority of God's Word and expose them for what they really are – dead ends of deception? We have seen in our time together, that the Bible teaches us that the cults are nothing but wide theological 'gates' and the 'easy way' that will eventually lead their followers to spiritual destruction, for the Word of God says, *"Enter by the narrow gate; for wide is the gate and broad is the way that leads to destruction, and there are many who go in by it. Because narrow is the gate and difficult is the way which leads to life, and there are few who find it."* (Matthew 7:13).

The cults are nothing but houses built upon the sands of misguided human teachings which will be eroded by the rains of time and even blown asunder by the winds of fickle human nature! They will ultimately be destroyed completely by the 'flood' of God's judgment – just like those destroyed by the 'judgement waters of Noah's Flood. The Word of God says, *"But everyone who hears these sayings of Mine, and does not do them, will be like a foolish man who built his house on the sand: and the rain descended, the floods came, and the winds blew and beat on that house; and it fell. And great was its fall."* (Matthew 7:26-27).

Cults are like waterless springs and mists driven by storms of dissension of which the Apostle Peter warned, *"These are wells without water, clouds carried by a tempest, for whom is reserved the blackness of darkness forever."* (2nd Peter 2:17).

Cults are the ones about which Christ spoke when He warned: *"If anyone does not abide in Me, he is cast out as a branch and is withered; and they gather them and throw them into the fire, and they are burned."* (John 15:6).

Ever since God planted His garden in Eden (Genesis 2:8), Satan the Devil has been trying to infiltrate and sow his parasitic cultic 'weeds' amongst 'the wheat' of God's people. In Matthew 13:25-30 the speaker says of this, *"Another parable He put forth to them, saying: "The kingdom of heaven is like a man who sowed good seed in his field; but while men slept, his enemy came and sowed tares among the wheat and went his way. But when the grain had sprouted and produced a crop, then the tares also appeared. So the servants of the owner came and said to him, 'Sir, did you not sow good seed in your field? How then does it have tares?' He said to them, 'An enemy has done this.' The servants said to him, 'Do you want us then to go and gather them up?' But he said, 'No, lest while you gather up the tares you also uproot the wheat with them. Let both grow together until the harvest, and at the time of harvest I will say to the reapers, "First gather together the tares and bind them in bundles to burn them, but gather the wheat into my barn."*

Soon after the church was inaugurated by the Holy Spirit descending like pillars of fire on the heads of the disciples on the Day of Pentecost, Satan again sought to nullify God's great harvest of souls by sowing 'tares'.[145] Tares of legalism, and of false

---

[145] *'tares'* are injurious weeds that in the early stages of growth look like a legitimate plant.

teachings amongst the 'wheat field' of God's children.

Just as the Apostle Paul sought to warn every man, *"Him we preach, warning every man and teaching every man in all wisdom, that we may present every man perfect in Christ Jesus"* (Colossians 1:28). So, we today must do all we can to 'save some by snatching them out of the burning' as the prophet Amos said, *"...you were like a firebrand plucked from the burning..."* (Chapter 4:11).

As Christians, we too need to be kept in check, as were the zealous servants who wanted to go out into the field and uproot the 'tares' from the 'wheat', lest we too uproot the good 'wheat' along with the parasitic 'tares'.

After doing all we can to help the cultist, if they don't respond, we must in finality, leave them in the hands of God. Sadly, if the deceived refuse to hear the truth, it is God who will settle the issue for all Eternity when what is called 'The Great White Throne Judgment' is conducted:

"Then I saw a great white throne and Him who sat on it, from whose face the earth and the heaven fled away. And there was found no place for them. And I saw the dead, small and great, standing before God, and books were opened. And an-other book was opened, which is the Book of Life. And the dead were judged according to their works, by the things which were written in the books. The sea gave up the dead who were in it, and Death and Hades delivered up the dead who were in them. And they were judged, each one according to his works. Then Death and Hades were cast into the lake of fire. This is the second death. And anyone not found written in the Book of Life was cast into the lake of fire..." (Chapter 20:11-15).

This is why Christ instructed us in the following parable of the Kingdom, to: *"Let both grow together until the harvest, and at the time of harvest I will say to the reapers, "First gather together the tares and* bind them in bundles to burn them, but gather the wheat into my barn." (Matthew 13:30).

As Christians, we should never seek to be exclusive or maintain strict conformity to the letter of law of the Bible rather than simply keeping the 'spirit of it'. If we did 'conform to the letter of the law, that would make us legalistic and we would be just like the cults. We should never make claims for Christ that He didn't make for Himself! Nor must we ever compromise the Biblical message of Christ in the face of theological heresy! Christ claimed to be the full and final revelation of God to mankind and the New Testament writers also attributed this uniqueness to Him, as it was stated in Colossians 1:19 & 2:9:

"For it pleased the Father that in Him all the fullness should dwell."

"For in Him dwells all the fullness of the Godhead bodily..."

The word used for 'fullness' above is the Greek word *'pleroma'* and it means "completion or, the totality of something". Here the Apostle Paul is insisting, in the face of false teaching, that in Christ the completeness of Deity[146], or Godhood, dwells in all its fullness. Jesus Christ was not merely endued in a special way with the Holy Spirit, as many cults would say, but is rather the dwelling-place for the very essence of God!

The Apostle Peter also affirmed this absolute uniqueness of the Lord Jesus Christ in his defence when he stood before Annas the high priest and to all who were of the high-priestly

---

[146] The word *'deity'* is another word for 'a god'. Or, a supernatural being that is supreme, holy, and in charge of creation or running life as we know it.

family when he said to them:

"Nor is there salvation in any other, for there is no other name under heaven given among men by which we must be saved." (Acts 4:12)

Therefore, whether we like it or not, no matter what anyone else tells you, this fact leaves out Confucius, Krishna, Maharaj Ji, Maharishi Mahesh Yogi, Mohammad, Baha'u'llah, Malcolm X, Mary Baker Eddy, Ellen G. White, Joseph Smith Jnr and Brigham Young, Charles and Myrtle Filmore, Elijah Mohammed, Herbert W. Armstrong and his son Garner Ted Armstrong, David Berg, Charles T. Russell and J.F. Rutherford and the Watchtower Governing Body, Victor Paul Wierwille, Rev. Sun Myung Moon, *et al!*

"Therefore God also has highly exalted Him [Jesus Christ] and given Him the name which is above every name, that at the name of Jesus every knee should bow, of those in heaven, and of those on earth, and of those under the earth, and that every tongue should confess that Jesus Christ is Lord, to the glory of God the Father". [Philippians 2:9-11; parenthesis added]

You are Invited to…

"Take him not only as your Saviour from the guilt of sin but also as your Saviour from the power of sin. He not only died to make atonement for your sins, he also rose again, and he lives today to set you free from the power of sin and to make intercession for you (Hebrews 7:25). Will you take him now as your deliverer from the power of sin? Will you come to this risen and mighty Lord Jesus with all your weakness and sins and trust him to set you free? That is the right thing to do with Jesus Christ: just take him as your Saviour, your crucified Saviour, from the guilt of sin and your risen Saviour from The power of sin."

— R.A. TORREY

CHAPTER TWENTY ONE

The Author's Short Story

It has been said by others that I have developed an incredibly wide knowledge of world religions, the cults, and the occult. All of which has come from my personal research and my own life experience. Barbara and I have developed a reputation for being tenacious in our desire to stand up and be counted when it comes to defending the Christian Faith!

I personally began to seriously study religion at the age of sixteen. This was due to my then Church of England (Anglican) minister telling me that the Bible, was "… something that only men like myself, who have been trained in theological college can understand"! Several days later and out of curiosity, I found and purchased a very thick paperback book at a newsagency with the title, *"The World's Religions"*! Without realising it way back then, it was that purchase that saw the beginning of what became for me a life-long study, which continues to this day!

In keeping with my interest and line of study, I have been awarded a Bachelor of Religious Education Degree (BR.Ed) for which I majored in Christian Apologetics[147] I studied with Jubilee International Bible College, Brisbane in the late 1980's. Subsequently, in August 2006, after two and a half years of intensive study, doing little else six days a week, I was presented with a Doctor of Divinity Degree (D.D.) from Master's International School of Divinity, Indiana USA.

In our younger days, Barbara and I were both active communicant members of the then Church of England - which has now become the Anglican Church of Australia. Our parents chose to attend separate churches in the same parish in Sydney. My family were fellowshipping at St John's and Barbara's family at St Marks. We were both involved in our respective Youth Groups. However, it was in the combined-church Youth Group meetings where we first got to know each other. At different times, we both learned our Catechisms and qualified to be Confirmed[148] by the church and we became communicant members.

I wanted to enlist in the Royal Australian Air Force (RAAF) as an apprentice after a Recruiting Exhibition visited my high school. However, my father was against the idea of me enlisting for 15 years! Three years of apprenticeship training,

---

[147] Christian apologetics is a field of Christian theology which aims to present a rational basis for the Christian faith, defending the faith against objections. ...

[148] Confirmation is the laying on of hands by the bishop with prayers for the gift of the Holy Spirit for mission and ministry. It is a time when baptised persons confirm the promises made on their behalf in infant baptism and take on adult responsibility for their Christian life. In the past confirmation occurred in the teenage years and allowed those confirmed to participate in Holy Communion. For further insight: http://www.anglican.org.au

followed by a further 12 years of service! Without telling my Dad, I went to the then Recruiting Centre at Rushcutters Bay, Sydney, where I made application to enlist when I turned 18 years of age. I completed all the aptitude and medical tests and was told I could enlist for period of six years as an Adult Trainee. However, I was still caught 'between a rock and a hard place' because I was still under the age of 21! When I asked my father for a second time, he refused again for the same reason – this time saying that six years was still far too long a time for someone my age to commit to!

Many years later, my Dad shared with me that his reluctance to allow me to enlist was a direct result of his own service with the RAAF where he served in New Guinea during WWII at Mylne Bay, Goodenough Island and Doba Dura. He really felt he could not be responsible for putting me in a position where the same dreadful things that happened to him could happen to me!

He became ill and was repatriated home from New Guinea after he was diagnosed as suffering from tuberculosis, malaria, epilepsy, and what was then called, 'War Neurosis'. Since about 1982 it has become known as Post Traumatic Stress Disorder, or PTSD! His health issues meant that he suffered debilitating and severe health problems throughout his life.

Why I made the effort to enlist in the RAAF a second time, was because I had been told 'on the quiet' by the Recruiting people that I could, at age 18 take court action to over-rule my Dad's refusal to allow me to enlist. However, it was during the intervening time that my wife to be, Barbara, came into the picture and we began 'going steady' (as it was called back then when a couple became inseparable from each other – now people just say they are, "In a relationship"!)

Barbara and I had known each other socially through our church youth fellowship for some years. It was Barbara who talked me out of taking legal action against my Dad - her advice to me was to wait until I was aged 21. Then I wouldn't need his permission! We married in 1959 and our relationship has stood the test of time - at the time of this writing we are coming up to our 55th Wedding Anniversary!

I think I had some help from my mother in convincing Dad that he should sign my papers for me, because, when visiting one weekend in early January1961, over Afternoon Tea, Dad asked Barbara if she approved of my intentions? She responded in the affirmative and said that I would enlist when I had my 21st Birthday in July! Dad looked at me and said, "Alright, get the enlistment papers and I'll sign them!" My recruit training began at RAAF Base Wagga Wagga[149], NSW, in April. Some said that I took to the Air Force life "like a duck takes to water"!

After my Marching Out Parade in June, at the conclusion of recruit training, I was posted to the School of Radio at Laverton, Victoria. On arrival, I was advised that there was an unknown waiting period, due to insufficient numbers, before I could start a course as a Telecommunication Technician. After some months of waiting, I learned that there were still only two of us waiting for a course. We had to wait unto they had another eight trainees a course could start. With no start date, I chose an alternative course and applied for further training at the RAAF School of Administration, which was back at Wagga! I graduated in February 1962 and was posted to No 2 Stores Depot at Regents Park, Sydney.

---

[149] Comonly known as 'Wagga'

In mid-April 1963 I was detached to RAAF Ubon, Thailand, for six months after winning a 'hat ballot' between myself and another who was also eligible to go. Ubon was located on the Laotian Border (about 300 miles East of Bangkok). I served there in support of No 79 Squadron's Sabre Jet Fighters. They were operating as a deterrent to Communist activities in Laos from North Vietnam. We were not aware of it at the time, but, this was the second phase of Australia's commitment during the early days of what was to escalate into the Vietnam War!

While based in Thailand I gained first-hand insights into the Buddhist religion. It was fascinating for me to live in a society where about 97% of the population were Buddhist. A Thai physician, Thongindra Pongsai, became a close friend. He was in charge of the World Health Organisation's Leprosy Control Project for the Ubon Province. Out of a provincial population of just over 100,000 at that time, he told me that he supervised the care of around 5,000 lepers! I spent a lot of time when off-duty discussing religion with him and the Pongsai family and Buddhist monks. I found their temples very interesting. They were like mini-museums with ancient and interesting artifacts on display.

On my return to Australia, I served at Headquarters Support Command, Melbourne, Victoria. I was involved in the conversion of the entire RAAF Stores Catalogue Numbering System to the NATO Stock Numbering System. This was the RAAF's initial computer uptake for their entire stores stock system.

In November 1965 I was promoted and posted to No 2 Aircraft Depot at Richmond, NSW. In early 1966 I responded to an invitation to apply for aircrew training as a loadmaster on the C130A Hercules transport aircraft of No 36 Squadron. In time I became Assistant to the Loadmaster Trainer and after several months, Loadmaster Trainer. After three years, during difficult times due to the wars in South-East Asia, I applied for discharge in September 1968. I was honourably discharged 'On Request' in late November. My flights had spanned Australia, New Zealand, Papua-New Guinea, Indonesia, Singapore, Malaysia, Borneo, Cocus Island, Thailand and South Vietnam. In every country I saw first-hand the practice of different religions, their rituals and various occult activities, which all added to my 'education'. My enquiring mind meant that I got to speak in-depth with the leaders and members of several Eastern religions.

The reader may ask what was Barbara doing during all this? She was doing what all good Service wives do - keeping the home fires burning and being a great mother to our then four young children, which in the next five years doubled in number to eight! We have five girls and three boys! At the time of this writing, we have 21 Grand-children and very soon four Great-Grandchildren!

My long involvement in South-East Asian conflicts and especially the war in South Vietnam – where I was flying in fresh troops, urgently needed equipment and supplies. Returning to Australia was the hard part as we transported the human wreckage of war back, both the wounded and the dead, from Vietnam – it began to take its toll on me.

Australia had become polarized as a nation, due to intense opposition to the war and military conscription. In addition, I had members of my family ostracizing me over the ethics of the War and my involvement in it – it all began to take its toll on me.

Our society, just like that of the USA, had become bitterly divided over the war in Vietnam! There were demonstrative

ANSWER TO THE CULT EXPLOSION

public protests with numerous rallies and huge 'Moratorium Marches' involving thousands of people, being held in our capital cities which didn't make things any easier for me! The Vietnam War was the subject of a hostile media campaign against the war. It seemed to be 'in my face' day and night 24/7! It was on the radio, front page news in the papers and even in my lounge room on TV! I have to ask the question, "What's new about the years of protest and resistance by the media against our troops serving and fighting, initially in Iraq and then Afghanistan, until just recently?"[150]

At the height of the Vietnam War, I was assigned to be crew on aircraft that supported the controversial visit to Australia in 1966 of the then US President, Lyndon B. Johnson. Our then prime minister, Harold Holt, became infamous with the media because of his public statement, "All the way with LBJ"! I transported the two main Commonwealth limousines used for his 'Welcome Street Parades'. Which were more like, 'You're Not Very Welcome' protests!

The Sydney Morning Herald newspaper, in an article by Alan Ramsey, published on 11th October 2003 said, "Half a million people lined Melbourne's streets for his motorcade. Almost as many cheered him in Sydney, [the] scene of the now celebrated incident in which the then NSW Liberal premier, Bob Askin, urged his driver to "Run over the b......s" after anti-Vietnam War protesters lay on the roadway in front of the President's car...". Our nation had never seen such huge protest

---

[150] As I write, a Task Force made up of various RAAF aircraft and several hundred RAAF and ARMY personnel have this week relocated to Qatar in the Middle East in response to the Islamic State threat in Iraq (initially it was ISIL, then ISIS, and now IS).

demonstrations and fortunately not since! Frequently, during the course of my off-duty life in the community, both in uniform and in civilian clothes, I was taken to task and verbally abused by strangers for participating in the war in Vietnam! Not only by people in the street, but as mentioned, by some members of my own family who bitterly opposed the war in Vietnam!

One of my experiences in South Vietnam is worth telling. In February 1968 my aircraft was conducting what we called a 'Milk-Run' operation to Phan-Rhang which occurred every 14 days. Our Canberra jet bombers were based there. On our arrival there our aircraft was immediately seconded to the USAF to fly village evacuation into a large American base at Cam-Rhan Bay.

No 36 Squadron Lockheed Hercules C130A

What we didn't know at the time was that it was the beginning of the largest military campaign of the war, which was launched by the Viet-Cong (VC) and the North Vietnamese Army (NVA) on January 30, 1968. It was designed to over-run the Allied Forces throughout the entire country in one massive attack. This intense battle is now known as 'The TET Offensive'[151]. After days of facing fierce opposition from the Allied Forces, both the VC and the NVA were defeated in the field.

However, what was won on the battle-front of TET was to be lost by the Allies on the media-front! It turned out to be a huge unexpected propaganda victory for the Communists! Journalists, with their frontline TV cameras showing the horror of war as it happened turned many against the war! The voice-overs were giving negative and sometimes lying commentary, directly into people's lounge rooms! Such 'adverse' publicity played directly into the hands of the 'anti-war protest movements' by giving them more 'grist for the mill' so to speak!

My involvement, especially during the TET Offensive, gave me first-hand insight into what man's inhumanity to man can do! I saw for the first time, how the war was affecting ordinary Vietnamese people. To see the elderly, men, women and children running desperately for their lives to get onto my aircraft in order to escape what would be certain death for them within hours was not at all pleasant – I felt sick inside afterwards! I had to sit them packed together on the metal floor of my aircraft - I was not equipped with centre seating on this trip. There were far too many people to even use the nylon-duralumin fold-down side seating! I sat them down in rows holding tie-down straps, which I rigged to each side of the aircraft, telling them to hold on with one hand and hold their children and meagre possessions with the other!

---

[151] For more detail see Appendix 5, 'The Tet Offensive".

Some of the women had chickens in small bamboo baskets, others carried piglets, others held articles of clothing and a variety of food containers and cooking utensils! It was impossible to count how many people we packed into our aircraft? When we did a short take-off from the dry rice paddies, it occurred to me that none of the people knew where they were going? When we got to Cam-Ranh Bay, as they left the aircraft, I realized, from the look of relief on their faces, they knew that if they had stayed in their village, they would have died that day!

I've said all that, to say this. It was the experiences of this trip that proved for me to be "the straw that broke the camel's back" emotionally. I could not reconcile in myself how a loving God would allow such things to happen to such innocent people? The vast majority of them had never asked for war! All they really wanted was to live their lives in peace.

As the result of being exposed to and being involved in war, I gradually lost whatever faith I had in God; my country for being involved; and for mankind's cruelty and brutality! To this day, I do not remember a single thing about the trip back home to from Cam-Rhan Bay to Australia! Nor do I remember anything of the many flights I made until the end of November 1968 when I was discharged.

My Section Leader and the Commanding Officer could see that I had become a troubled man. They knew that I was drinking too much. What I didn't realise at the time was that I was using alcohol to 'self-medicate' in order to block out the pain of the anxious and worrying thoughts that were continually flooding into my mind.

Candidates for a Cult!

Experiences like those I mentioned and many others, had the

effect of 'blindly setting up' both myself and Barbara to accept the false gospel of the Jehovah's Witnesses (JW's) when it came along! When they first called in July 1968, it was the Vietnam War issue that the JW's raised with me. I have to admit, they immediately got my attention! They spoke about their opposition to war and not being involved in any war effort at all. This was a statement and an issue for which I had come to so desperately want to hear from someone with authority.

Because I felt that God had gone 'missing in action' in Vietnam I had wanted someone to tell me for quite some time, that war was wrong and therefore it must be Biblically wrong! At that point in time all of the authority figures in my life, some family members, close friends, two RAAF chaplains, my government (who sent us to war) and various church ministers with whom I had consulted seeking help, were all supportive of the war! I could see for myself that the Vietnam War was literally going nowhere. In my mind, the former authority figures in my life had lost any credibility that I once thought they had!

One has to admit that the JW's and members of similar religious groups do seem to speak with authority - but, as our research has proven, it's only evident on their pet subjects! Barbara resisted joining the JW's initially, but sadly was eventually persuaded by some very strong and committed JW women that their 'way' was the right and the only 'true way' to go. No doubt, with hindsight, Barbara was influenced by the seeming 'new husband' that she now had! I had stopped both drinking and smoking excessively and had cleaned up my act, so to speak.

So, Barbara and I joined with the JW's and we were both eventually baptised by immersion in water by them. Despite what we had been taught by them, about the significance of our water baptism, we soon found out, that it only entitled us to be called, 'Kingdom Publishers'! Which meant that we were now were obligated to knock on doors selling Watchtower Books, Watchtower Bibles, Watchtower and Awake Magazines. All of which we had to purchase first! At our water baptism we actually placed ourselves under the authority of the local congregation's elders[152]. As a result, we spent the next ten years of their lives being influenced and controlled in every area of our lives!

I personally believe that for me, it was the effects of what was to be eventually diagnosed as suffering from the war-caused illness of Post-Traumatic Stress Disorder, or PTSD, which prevented me at the time, from having a clear mind and the ability to think clearly and fully investigate the roots of the JW's and their Watchtower Bible and Tract Society when they first contacted me!

In time I collected and got to read many of their older books and magazines.[153] I began learning of their deceptions and cover-ups over many years! Like the many false dates for their 'end of the world predictions' of 1874, 1914, 1916, 1918, 1925, 1935, 1942 (there was some talk around 1957 when the Russians launched Sputnik – it was said to be 'a sign and a wonder in the Heavens'!) and their now failed embarrassing prediction for

---

[152] Until a newly associated person is trained to learn and answer certain questions and is baptized in water by them, they are only known loosely as, "Associated Ones" and the elders have no authority over them. They can leave any time they want to, with some opposition of course. However, water baptised Jehovah's Witnesses cannot resign and leave, they have to be excommunicated, or disfellowshipped as they call it!

[153] An elderly and long-serving Jehovah's Witness, with whom I had become friends, without me knowing, had instructed his family that when he passed away that I was to be given all of his JW books and Watchtower and Awake magazines. Many of them dated back to the 1930's and 1940's.

October 1975! I also discovered voluminous changes in their teachings over the years. Once again I began to feel that the bottom was falling out of my life!

Walking into a Kingdom Hall one Sunday afternoon, with my family, in 1973 I believe that the True God actually spoke to me, in a spontaneous thought, *"Fred, you no longer believe what these people believe. It would be hypocritical for you to continue with them"*! Suddenly I realised that it was true, I no longer could accept what the JW's had taught me to believe! I knew at that point that to continue to as a member of the JW's would be insincere on my part. If I did I would be a pretender! So, that coming week I completed all my JW paperwork and resigned from my congregational positions and left! The elders tried to change my mind, but couldn't. I was branded by the elders and others as a having become a 'backslidden husband and father'! Initially, my wife and family saw me in that same vein.

My leaving the Jehovah's Witnesses was only two years before what was yet to become another of their failed dates for 'the Battle of Armageddon' and the end of 'this world's system of things' as we knew it in 1975! The JW's had been taught by their leaders since 1968 that 'the Battle of Armageddon' was to begin on the 14-15th October 1975! For me to resign just before that date, in the minds of all of my former JW so-called 'friends' and those of my congregation, meant in their minds, that what I had done was incredibly and absolutely foolish and I would not survive 1975!

During my involvement with the JW's I held several of the ministerial positions at Congregation level, including that of Theocratic Ministry School Servant (which was normally an elder's role). As such I was teaching them the art of public speaking and how to conduct themselves at your door! I was a guest speaker to other congregations and spoke at several Circuit Conventions. I served on special projects with the Australian Watchtower Society's headquarters staff, which was then based at Strathfield, in Sydney.

Barbara and the children chose not to follow my actions and we were to enter into a very difficult time as husband and wife. My status with the JW's was that of, 'Backslidden Husband and Father"! My older children of course were devastated.

I had again stepped into what I now call, "My Second Spiritual Void"! My first 'void' occurred when driving through the main gate at Richmond RAAF Base for the last time the day I was discharged in late November 1968 – it felt surreal, it was as if I had driven into a vacuum of nothingness?

I became tired and bored of sitting around home by myself when the family were attending the compulsory five JW meetings on three days of each week. Having no friends outside the JW's meant that I soon sheepishly and secretly returned to some of my old pre-JW habits and ways. After all, if the JW's were right with their date this time, I was going to die at Armageddon on October 14-15th 1975! Because of their 'Soul Sleep' teaching, I would be conscious of nothing! That's why I knew I had no future at all. I became a heavy drinker and became involved in many things that I now feel nothing but shame for. Sadly, many of those 'things' are now deemed to be acceptable by our society.

The result of my poor conduct was that I almost lost my wife and family. The JW elders were encouraging my wife to leave me. However, thanks to the grace and providence of God, His hand was still upon my life, without me even knowing it at the time. This, coupled with the prayers of my Christian family members, led me, in spite of my then heavily burdened state of mind, to continue my ongoing research into the 'mysterious' beginnings and teachings of the JW's. In my thinking I desperately needed to prove them wrong in every area of their teachings and practices for myself. I studied in depth the failed dates and the roots of their ever-changing teachings. I concluded finally that there was absolutely no way they could possibly be right and be the only organisation that God was dealing through on earth today! It was those studies that led me to begin researching other religions as I still believed that I really had to find out which one was the true religion!

As a JW I did not realise that I had been serving the 'wrong jesus' (or a 'false christ') as mentioned earlier. But, on Easter Sunday, 1978 my relationship with the real Lord Jesus Christ was restored. I say "restored" because I had already accepted Jesus Christ as my Lord and Saviour in November 1957!

Sadly, like it has been for many folk, at that time there was no one who made themselves available to disciple me and teach me the basics of my newfound Christian faith. I've never seen the person who lead me to Christ again! In time the broken family relationships with my alienated relatives were restored. I had been taught by the JW's that they all 'belonged to the devil' and so I had to avoid them – I would have been disciplined in some way if I hadn't!

Barbara and the children eventually came to see a more dramatic change in my lifestyle and character, after my repentance and return to the real Christian Faith. I once again stopped drinking, smoking, gambling and hanging out with the wrong people for a second time! Within twelve months (this is another story), both she and the seven children we had then, finally left the JW's and the older ones became Born-again Christians also!

A few months after the family stopped fellowshipping with the JW's, our eldest daughter – who had naturally become confused in herself due to all my up and downs - was encouraged by the family members of a former JW girlfriend to, "...leave home and come back and remain loyal to Jehovah's Organisation so that you and your brothers and sisters will get through the Battle of Armageddon in 1975"!

She was told by JW elders, "It's not good to be worrying about your Mum and Dad now that they are outside Jehovah's Ark of Safety" (meaning that to them we were not Jehovah's Witnesses anymore) the important thing for you now is, as the eldest of the family, you have to take the responsibility of staying loyal to God's organisation in order to save both yourself and your brothers and sisters!"

Believing that she was doing the right thing, she discretely left home. The JW family who encouraged her to leave, were the very ones we had gotten to love. We related for many years and had many enjoyable times together. They had the audacity to lie to us when we approached them and questioned them as to our daughter's whereabouts!

The Jehovah's Witnesses had forbidden her to have any contact with us. Her 'new family' lied to a NSW Police officer who volunteered to call on the home we thought she was staying in. She was to tell us a year later that she was actually hiding in a bedroom when we called! The Police could not officially, or legally, help as she was then over 18 years-of-age. The police made the point that she was with them of her own will. So their hands were tied.

During her time with the JW's our daughter said the JW family she stayed with tried unsuccessfully to marry her off to eligible young JW males who they invited home for meals! Thankfully our prayers for her were answered (yet another story!) and she came home of her own volition, almost year after she had left! All our family members who had been baptised in water by the JW's, were disfellowshipped by the elders without any of us knowing a thing about it! We became aware of the action taken by the local leaders when our second daughter was told, by her former close JW girlfriend, "Oh, I shouldn't be talking to you, you know you've been disfellowshipped don't you?"

Contrary to what cult members will tell you, there is Good News! That is that there is life after being involved with a cult! In our experience when one gives one's heart to Jesus Christ and is Born-again, that as the Bible says, 'the old person' certainly does pass away in time and a new one has come!

All those years of working and toiling to attend five meetings a week, attending compulsory conventions locally, state and interstate, and spending thousands of hours knocking on doors selling Watchtower publications, all at our own expense, has really paid off for us. How so you may ask?

From our experience, even though grievous at the time, we have a 'deposit' of first-hand knowledge and experiences that we are able to draw from frequently in order to help and assist others. This happens when we are called on to help others to come out of, or avoid getting into, spiritual bondage and be entangled in the webs of deception of authoritarian mind-numbing cults. Our experience immediately tells when we begin to share with others because they quickly understand that we are credibile people because we've been through exactly what they are going through!

This writing represents some of our experience, research,

and many years of counselling others who have been attacked by the 'ravenous wolves' mentioned in Matthew 7:15! Today, to actually be a part of what God is doing in the lives of thousands of people throughout the world is truly a blessing and a great privilege. There is absolutely no comparison between the joy of knowing the love, forgiveness and the grace of God and being lost in the legalistic bondage of a false religion or cult! We trust that you will never ever have to go through the agony of deceit and abuse that we have been through. It would be true to say that only in Jesus Christ have we been liberated from the past. To know and proclaim Him is our motive for what we do – and that is we willingly choose to be 'the warning sign at the top of the cliff' to others so to speak, than to be 'the ambulance at the bottom' picking up the human wreckage created by false religion and the dangerous cults!

      Don't get involved in practicing unsafe sects!

APPENDICES

APPENDIX ONE

TEN SIGNALS THAT SAY,
"YOU ARE NOT WELCOME IN THIS CHURCH"

ARTICLE BY JOE MCKEEVER

"You shall love (the stranger) as yourself, for you were strangers in the land of Egypt" (Leviticus 19:34).

As a retired pastor who preaches in a different church almost every Sunday, a fun thing I get to do is study the church bulletins (or handouts or worship guides) which everyone receives on entering the building. You can learn a great deal about a church's priorities and personality in five minutes of perusing that sheet.

As an outsider - that is, not a member or regular here - I get to see how first-timers read that material and feel something of the same thing they feel. I become the ultimate mystery shopper for churches. That is not to say that I pass along all my (ahem) insights and conclusions to pastors. Truth be told, most leaders do not welcome judgments from visitors on what they are doing and how they can do it better. So, unless asked, I keep it to myself.

Now, in all fairness, most churches are eager to receive newcomers and want them to feel at home and even consider joining. And the worship bulletins reflect that with announcements of after-benediction receptions to meet the pastors, the occasional luncheon for newcomers to learn about the church and get their questions answered, and free materials in the foyer. Now, surely all the other churches want first-timers to like them and consider joining. No church willingly turns its nose up at newcomers, at least none that I know of. But that is the effect of our misbehavior. Here are ten ways churches signal newcomers they are not wanted:

1. The front door is locked. One church where I was to preach has a lovely front facade which borders on the sidewalk. The front doors are impressive and stately. So, after parking to the side of the building, I did what I always do: walked to the front and entered as a visitor would. Except I didn't go in. The doors were locked. All of them. After walking back around the side and entering from the parking lot, I approached an usher and asked about the locked door.

"No one comes in from that entrance," he said. "The parking lot is to the side."

I said, "What about walk-ins? People from the neighborhood who come across the street."

He said, "No one does that."

He's right. They stay away because the church has told them they're not welcome. One church I visited had plate glass doors where the interior of the lobby was clearly visible from the front steps. A table had been shoved against the doors to prevent anyone from entering that way. I did not ask why; I knew. The parking lot was in the rear. Regulars parked back there and entered through those doors. That church, in a constant struggle for survival, is its own worst enemy. They might as well erect a sign in front of the church that reads, "First-timers unwelcome."

2. The functioning entrance is opened late. Even if we understand why a rarely used front door is kept locked, it makes

no sense that the primary door should be closed. And yet, I have walked up to an entrance clearly marked and found it locked. The pastor explained, "We unlock it 15 minutes prior to the service."

If that pastor is a friend and we already have a solid relationship, I will say something gracious, like, "What? Are you out of your cotton-picking mind? A lot of people like to come early. Seniors do. First-timers like to get there early to see the lay of the land. That door ought to be unlocked a minimum of 45 minutes prior to the announced worship time." If the pastor and I are meeting for the first time, I'll still make the point, although a little gentler than that.

3. The church news gives inadequate information. The announcement reads: "The youth will have their next meeting this week at Stacy's house. See Shawn for directions. Team B is in charge of refreshments." Good luck to the young person visiting that day and hoping to break into the clique. He has no idea who Shawn is, how to get to Stacy's house or what's going on if he dares to attend. So, the youth does not return. Next Sunday, he tries that church across town that is drawing in great crowds of teens. For good reason, I imagine. They act like they actually want them to come.

4. The pulpit is unfriendly to first-timers. The pastor says, "I'm going to call on Bob to lead the prayer." Or, "Now, Susan will tell us about the women's luncheon today." "Tom will be at the front door with information on the project." By not using the full names of people, the pastor ends up speaking only to insiders. Outsiders enter without knowing anyone and leave the same way.

5. The congregation sends its own signals. Is visitor's parking clearly marked? And when you park there, does someone greet you with a warm welcome and helpful information? Or, do

you find a parking place wherever you can and receive only stares as you approach the entrance? Did you get the impression that you were sitting in someone else's pew today?

Did anyone make an effort to learn your name and see if you have a question? Or, was the only handshake you received given during the in-service time as announced in the bulletin? (Those, incidentally, do not count when assessing the friendliness of a congregation. Only spontaneous acts of kindness count.)

This week, a pastor and I had lunch at a diner in downtown New Orleans which I've visited only once and he not at all. We were amused at some of the signs posted around the eatery. One said rather prominently, "Guests are not to stay beyond one hour." My friend Jim laughed, "I guess they're saying we shouldn't dawdle."

Churches have their own signs, although not as clear or blatant as that. Usually, they are read in the faces, smiles (or lack of one), and tone of voice of members.

6. The insider language keeps outsiders away. Now, I'm not one who believes we should strip all our worship service prayers and hymns and sermons of all references to sanctification, the blood, justification, atonement, and such. This is who we are. However, when we use the terms without a word of explanation--particularly, if we do it again and again--first-timers unaccustomed to the terms feel the same way you would if you dropped in on a foreign language class mid-semester: lost.

We signal visitors that they are welcome in our services when we give occasional explanations to our terms and customs which they might find strange.

7. No attempt is made to get information on visitors. Now, most church bulletins which I see from week to week have the

perforated tear-off which asks for all kinds of information and even gives people ways to sign up for courses or dinners. But I've been amazed at how many do not ask for that information. So, a visitor comes and goes. The church had one opportunity to reach out to him or her and blew it.

A church which is successful in reaching people for Christ will use redundancy. That is, they will have multiple methods for engaging newcomers, everything from greeters in the parking lot to friendly ushers to attractive bulletins and after-service receptions.

8. No one follows up on first-timers. One of the ministers of my church helped me with this. He said, "Asking people to fill out a guest card implies that there will be some kind of contact with them afterwards." He pointed out that our pastor informs them "No salesman will call," but even so, "Someone phones many visitors and letters go out to most." The first-timer who visits a church and does everything right has a right to expect some kind of follow-up from a leader of that congregation. We're frequently told that people today cherish their privacy and do not want to give their name and contact information until they decide this church is trustworthy. My response to that is: it's true, but not universally true. Many people still want to be enthusiastically welcomed and will respond to invitations to be given the grand tour and taken to lunch afterwards. In most cases leaders can tell from guest cards whether a visit will be welcomed. If not, at the very least a phone call should be made. If the caller receives an answering machine, he/she leaves the message and may decide this is sufficient for the first time. (Every situation is different. There are few hard and fast rules. Ask the Holy Spirit to lead you.)

9. Intangibles often send the signals loud and clear. In one

church I served, a couple roamed the auditorium before and after services in search of anyone they did not know. Lee and Dottie Andrews greeted the newcomers, engaged them in conversation, and quickly determined if an invitation to lunch would be in order. Almost every Sunday, they hosted a visiting family at the local cafeteria. At least half of these joined our church.

In another church, a husband and wife who sold real estate brought their clients to church with them. Some of the most active and faithful members who joined during my years in that church were introduced by Bob and Beth Keys.

Often, it's nothing more than a great smile that seals the deal. Or a warm, genuinely friendly handshake. A friendly, "Hey, have you found everything you need here?" may be all that's needed. Some churches install a newcomer's desk in the foyer, where visitors can meet knowledgeable leaders, pick up material, and get questions answered. Those can be great, but there is one caveat: you must have the right people on that desk. Individuals gifted with great smiles and servant spirits and infinite patience are ideal.

10. What happens following the service can make the difference. You the newcomer have enjoyed the service, you were blessed by the sermon, and you would like to greet the pastor and begin an acquaintance with this church. Most churches are set up for you to do just this. But not all. I've been in churches where within 5 minutes after the benediction, the place was deserted. People were so eager to leave, they hardly spoke to one another, much less guests. The signal they send the visitor is clear: "We don't care for our church and you wouldn't either."

Healthy church congregations love each other and welcome newcomers and their people are reluctant to leave following the end of services. One wonders if pastors and other leaders realize just how scary it can be for a person new in the city to venture into an unfamiliar church. It is an act of courage of the first dimension.

The Lord told Israel to reach out to newcomers and welcome them. After all, they themselves knew what it was to live in a strange country where the language and customs were foreign and they were missing home. God wanted Israel to remember always how that felt so they would welcome the stranger within their gates. How much more should a church of the Lord Jesus Christ?

Used with permission from the Author.
Joe's articles can be found at www.joemckeever.com

A SAFE GROUP, CHURCH, OR LEADER...

Will willingly answer your questions satisfactorily
Will willingly disclose information to you
Relates to and supports the principles of democracy
Will not vilify or ex-communicate former members
Will not have a negative paper trail (court cases, negative personal news articles, police record, etc.)
Will encourage communication with your existing friendships
Will recognize reasonable boundaries and limitations
Will encourage 'Critical Thinking', individual autonomy and self-esteem
Will admit mistakes and accept constructive criticism
Will not be the only source of knowledge and learning

You should trust your 'gut instinct' about people and groups

APPENDIX TWO

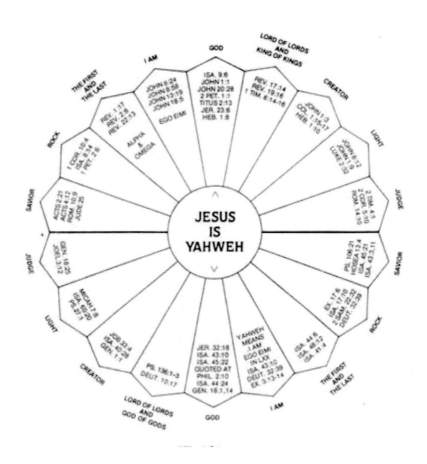

The 'Jesus is Yahweh' wheel, Cetnar, W.I. & J., 1983, "Questions for Jehovah's Witnesses," Bill (now deceased) & Joan Cetnar: Kunkletown PA, Reprinted from the back cover.

APPENDIX THREE

THE SEVENTH-DAY ADVENTIST 'CLEAR WORD BIBLE', JESUS, AND MICHAEL THE ARCHANGEL

The Seventh Day Adventists (SDA's) teach that Jesus and Michael the Archangel are one and the same (in spite of what they tell you they believe today!). However, some people mistakenly think that the SDA's are teaching that Jesus is a created angel and therefore not truly divine. But that is not the Seventh-day Adventist position. Instead, they are saying that the Old Testament manifestation of Michael the Archangel was actually the pre-incarnate Christ and that he is not created. They are incorrect in their comparison, but in it they are not denying the deity of Christ. Notice the difference in the following examples:

The New American Standard Bible (NASB – a recognised translation) says in john 8:58, "Jesus said to them, "Truly, truly, I say to you, before Abraham was born, I am." However, the SDA clear word bible (CWB – which is a paraphrase by hand version by one Jack J. Blanco [154]) says, Jesus answered, "Because I existed before Abraham was born."! Comment: this is a problem because the Greek *ego eimi* used here literally means, "I AM." The Jews wanted to kill Jesus for saying these words because it was so reflective of Exodus 3:14 where god says his name is "I AM".(see John 10:30-33 for confirmation of this). The SDA's changed their belief in recent years and now affirm the Deity of Christ, but

---

[154] Former Dean of the School of Religion of Southern Adventist University, near Chattanooga, Tennessee, USA

changing this is quite odd and is more in line with the Jehovah's Witness version than that of the true Biblical Jesus!

Compare, John 10:30 *"I and the Father are one."*(NASB). In the SDA CWB it is rendered, "You see, my Father and I are so close, we're one". Comment: This is a bad rendition because Jesus' oneness with God is not based on their closeness, but solely on their nature. Jesus is by nature both human and divine. In Theological circles, this is called the Hypostatic Union.

Also compare: 1 Thess. 4:16 *"For the Lord Himself will descend from heaven with a shout, with the voice of the archangel and with the trumpet of God, and the dead in Christ will rise first."* (NASB). In the SDA CWB it states, "When Christ descends from heaven as the Archangel, He will give a shout like a trumpet, which is God's call to the dead, and those who died in Christ will rise first." Comment: The Seventh Day Adventist theology comes shining through in this alteration, which is more commentary than anything else. The SDA church's 'Messenger' (or Prophet, Ellen G. White) taught that Jesus is Michael the Archangel; hence, why they change the meaning of the text, to make it fit their theology. This is not good - we should let the Bible speak for itself!

Now note, Jude 9,*"But Michael the archangel, when he disputed with the devil and argued about the body of Moses, did not dare pronounce against him a railing judgment, but said, "The Lord rebuke you!"* (NASB) In the CWB, "In contrast to these ungodly men is the Lord Jesus, also called Michael the Archangel, for He is over the entire angelic host. When He was challenged by Satan about His intentions to resurrect Moses, He didn't come at Satan with a blistering attack, nor did He condemn him with mockery. He simply said, "God rebuke you for claiming Moses' body." Comment: This is another example of the SDA long-standing theology governing their paraphrase. Biblically speaking, Jesus is definitely not Michael the Archangel! They are separate and this combining of them is an error which is reflected in their modification of the text. Finally, compare, Rev. 12:7 *"And there was war in heaven, Michael and his angels waging war with the dragon. The dragon and his angels waged war..."* (NASB) In the SDA CWB, "This controversy between God and the dragon began years ago in heaven. God's Son Michael and the loyal angels fought against the dragon and his angels." Comment: Notice again how the theology that Jesus and Michael the Archangel are one and the same comes through in this verse, but that is not what it is saying!

Sighted and copied from http://carm.org/clear-word-bible-jesus-michael 2 Sep 2014

APPENDIX FOUR

THE GREEK PREPOSITION *'EN'* CHART

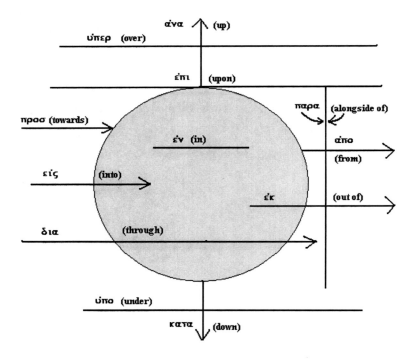

ANSWER TO THE CULT EXPLOSION

APPENDIX FIVE

THE GREEK PREPOSITION 'EN' ILLUSTRATION

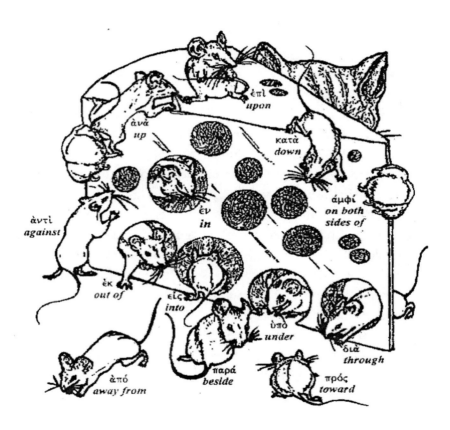

APPENDIX SIX

Vietnam War - Tet Offensive

The following is offered in order to perhaps give some understanding as to how one gradually, over time, becomes a 'candidate for a cult'?

The South Vietnam War Tet Offensive, launched in early 1968 by the Viet Cong, marked a significant escalation in the scale and the intensity of the War. Although it was defeated in a strict military sense, the Tet Offensive shook the resolve of the Americans and their allies in Vietnam, and fuelled anti-war sentiment in America, Australia and the rest of the world.

In 1967 factions within the South Vietnamese Viet Cong and North Vietnamese leadership began to call for a change of direction in the war's conduct. General Vo Nguyen Giap, who had formerly advocated waging a largely guerrilla type war, came to believe a "quick victory" might now be possible. Planning therefore began for a major offensive in South Vietnam that would provoke a "general uprising" against the corrupt and unpopular South Vietnamese Government. Abandoning conventional military wisdom, Viet Cong forces were not heavily concentrated for the offensive. The aim, instead, was to mount as many different attacks in as many locations as possible. In a departure from traditional guerrilla tactics, the main targets were in population centres rather than the countryside.

The offensive, during which more than 100 towns and cities were attacked, began during the early hours of 31 January 1968. The first assaults achieved almost complete surprise, not least because they occurred over the Chinese New Year or Tet holiday period, which, according to recent tradition, was a time of truce. In many places the Viet Cong were astonishingly successful; in the former capital, Hue, they took control of a large part of the city. The most spectacular Viet Cong successes were, however, in the South Vietnamese capital of Saigon, where a number of government buildings were attacked. An elite Viet Cong squad even managed to fight its way into the grounds of the American Embassy.

Although most of the attacks were quickly defeated, in Hue and at the American provincial base at Khe Sahn, Tet signaled the beginning of protracted battles. However, there was no "general uprising" in South Vietnam. The "quick victory" had turned into a disastrous defeat and recriminations within the communist leadership soon followed. With the Viet Cong decimated, General Giap lost much of his authority, ultimately being retained merely in the figurehead role of Minister of Defence. Only much later would the Viet Cong and North Vietnamese realise what they had actually achieved.

The Tet Offensive shocked the Americans and their allies, especially because it occurred at a time when they thought they were winning the war. Graphic footage of fighting in Saigon and Hue was broadcast into American households and around the world. The bitterness and desperation conveyed in these images deeply affected many people – even those who had until then broadly supported American involvement in Vietnam. The initial Viet Cong successes, the ferocity of the fighting and heavy American and South Vietnamese casualties ultimately left a far greater impression on worldwide public opinion than the offensive's final defeat.

After the Tet Offensive American politicians and military leaders doubted whether a military victory would be possible, and began to think of other ways of ending the conflict. In this sense Tet marks the turning point in the Vietnam War. But perhaps the Offensive's most enduring significance lay in how widely it revealed the horrors of the Vietnam War and indeed war in general.

---

http://vietnam-war.commemoration.gov.au/
Accessed 28 Aug 2014

APPENDIX SEVEN

Religions that Deny the Doctrine of the Trinity

The doctrine of the Trinity is central to most Christian denominations and faith groups, although not all. The term "Trinity" is not found in the Bible and is a concept of Christianity that for many is not easy to grasp or explain. Yet most evangelical Bible scholars agree that the Trinity doctrine is clearly expressed within the Scriptures.

The following faith groups and religions are among those that reject the doctrine of the Trinity. Some of the groups mentioned here are mentioned elsewhere in this book. However, what I am emphasising here is their non-belief in the Trinity! The list is not exhaustive but encompasses several of the major groups and religious movements. Included is a brief explanation of each group's beliefs about the nature of God, revealing a deviation from the doctrine of the Trinity.

For comparison purposes, the biblical Trinity doctrine is defined as follows: "There is only one God, made up of three distinct Persons who exist in co-equal, co-eternal communion as the Father, Son and Holy Spirit."

Mormonism or The Latter-day Saints: Founded By: Joseph Smith, Jr., 1830. Mormons believe that God has a physical, flesh and bones, eternal, perfect body. Men have the potential to become gods as well. Jesus is God's literal son, a separate being from God the Father and the "elder brother" of men. The Holy Spirit is also a separate being from God the Father and God the Son. The Holy Spirit is regarded as an impersonal power or spirit being. These three separate beings are "one" only in their purpose, and they make up the Godhead.

Seventh-day Adventists: Most Christians are amazed to learn that the SDA's, since early days in the mid-1800's, believed that Jesus Christ is Michael the Archangel! This heresy was brought to them by Mrs Ellen G. White, who was then and still is their "Messenger" (read 'prophet'). She claimed 'heavenly revelation' for the teaching while in a trance! In recent years the SDA's say they have changed this teaching and now believe in Jesus's Deity! They should also reject her as their *"Spirit of Prophecy"*[155] (Chapter 17). If they did that, then they could not possibly be, "the end-time Remnant Church" as she and they claim! Obviously, they hold openly that Jesus is God the Son, and hide from you that he is also Michael! In fact, Ellen White <u>denied</u> the deity of Jesus, when in 1903 she said, "The man Christ Jesus was not the Lord God Almighty"[156]. However, today's SDA's claim they believe that Jesus is part of the Godhead and in their official statement of faith (See footnote #150 Chapters 2 &4). Remember, until recent years SDA's denied Jesus' deity saying He was only an archangel! Their Commentary, volume 5, pg. 1129, cites Ellen White as saying..."The man Christ Jesus was not the Lord God Almighty."[157] If you've got the wrong Jesus? Then you lose!

Jehovah's Witnesses: Said to be founded By: Charles Taze

---

[155] SDA Book, 'Seventh-day Adventists Believe...27 A Biblical Exposition of Fundamental Doctrines', Chapters 2,4,17, The Gift of Prophecy, pages 217-229
[156] http://www.jesus-is-savior.com   Accessed and sighted 1 Sep 2014
[157] Ellen G. White (1903, ms 150, SDA; Commentary V, p. 1129

Russell, 1879. Succeeded by Joseph F. Rutherford, 1917. Jehovah's Witnesses believe that God is one person, Jehovah. Jesus was Jehovah's first creation. Jesus is not God, nor part of the Godhead. He is higher than the angels, but inferior to God. Jehovah used Jesus to create the rest of the universe. Before Jesus came to earth he was known as the archangel Michael. The Holy Spirit is an impersonal force from Jehovah, but not God.

Christian Science: Founded by: Mary Baker eddy, 1879. Christian Scientists (neither Christian, not Scientific!) believe the trinity is life, truth and love. As an impersonal principle, god is the only thing that truly exists. Everything else (matter) is an illusion. Jesus, though not god, is the son of god. He was the promised messiah but was not a deity. The holy spirit is divine science in the teachings of christian science.

Armstrongism: (the Philadelphia Church of God, the Global Church of God, the United Church of God). Founded by: Herbert W. Armstrong, 1934. Traditional Armstrongism denies a trinity, defining god as "a family of individuals." Original teachings say jesus did not have a physical resurrection and the holy spirit is an impersonal force.

Christadelphians: Founded by: Dr. John Thomas, 1864. They believe god is one indivisible unity, not three distinct persons existing in one god. They deny the Divinity of Jesus, believing he is fully human and separate from god. They do not believe the Holy Spirit is the third person of the Trinity, but is simply a force—the "unseen power" from god. They do not believe that

Satan the Devil even exists!

Oneness Pentecostals: Founded By: Frank Ewart, 1913. Oneness Pentecostals believe that there is one God and God is one. Throughout time God manifested himself in three ways or "forms" (not persons), as Father, Son and Holy Spirit. Oneness Pentecostals take issue with the Trinity doctrine chiefly for its use of the term "person." They believe God cannot be three distinct persons, but only one being who has revealed himself in three different modes. It is important to note that Oneness Pentecostals do affirm the deity of Jesus Christ and the Holy Spirit.

Unification Church: Founded By: Sun Myung Moon, 1954. Unification adherents believe that God is positive and negative, male and female. The universe is God's body, made by him. Jesus was not God, but a man. He did not experience a physical resurrection. In fact, his mission on earth failed and will be fulfilled through Sun Myung Moon, who is greater than Jesus. The Holy Spirit is feminine in nature. She collaborates with Jesus in the spirit realm to draw people to Sun Myung Moon.

Unity School Of Christianity: Founded By: Charles And Myrtle Fillmore, 1889. Similar to Christian Science, unity adherents believe god is an unseen, impersonal principle, not a person. God is a force within everyone and everything. Jesus was only a man, not the Christ. He simply realized his spiritual identity as the Christ by practicing his potential for perfection. This is something all men can achieve. Jesus did not resurrect from the dead, but rather, he reincarnated. The Holy Spirit is the active expression of god's law. Only the spirit part of us is real, matter is not real.

Scientology – Dianetics: Founded in 1954 by former science fiction writer, before WWII, Ron L. Hubbard. Scientology defines god as being dynamic infinity. Jesus is not god, savior or creator, nor does he have control of supernatural powers. He is usually overlooked in Dianetics. The Holy Spirit is absent from this belief system as well. Men are claimed to be "thetan" i.e., immortal, spiritual beings with limitless capabilities and powers, though often they are unaware of this potential? Scientology teaches men how to achieve the "higher states of awareness and ability" through practicing Dianetics, at great cost to the individual.

See footnotes below for sources[158]

---

[158]

1. Cults, World Religions and the Occult by Kenneth Boa
2. Christianity, Cults & Religions (Chart) by Rose Publishing
3. Religious Tolerance.org
4. Christian Apologetics and Research Ministry

NOTES

For further information and insights about many other false teachings and the various cults, visit our website at:

http://mandateministries.com.au

Other writings by Fred Grigg:

Who's Minding Us – the New Age Movement?
The Masonic Mirage
The Adventist Puzzle
The Rapture
The Jehovah's Witnesses
The Christadelphians
The Deception of Martial Arts and Yoga
Islam
The Battle to Pray
Who's Calling?

Mandate Ministries
Gold Coast, Australia

ABOUT THE AUTHOR

Fred Grigg

Fred served in the RAAF and became a Vietnam and South-East Asian War Veteran. His service eventually affected him so much that it led him and his family into ten years of servitude, from 1968-1978, with the Jehovah's Witnesses (JW's).

Discovering the JW's had the wrong 'jesus' and their 'roots' were riddled with false prophesies, he resigned in 1971. It took another seven years before his wife and family decided to leave them for much the same reason! He worked for the Anglo-Australian Telescope, at Coonabarabran, NSW. One of his two roles was that of Night Assistant (or, Telescope Operator). This was where and how he gained his knowledge of the stars and the heavens. He worked with numerous astronomers from several nations. Many of them were Christians.

He has several years of pastoral experience and many years of itinerant ministry teaching the Word and exposing dangerous religious groups. He received a Bachelor of Religious Education Degree from Jubilee International Bible College, Brisbane. Years later, after further studying for two and a half years, he was presented with his Doctorate of Divinity Degree from Master's International School of Divinity, Indiana, USA. He is a member of the Australian Society of Authors.

He, and his wife Barbara, are dedicated to teaching and equipping the Body of Christ, not only about dangerous religious groups, but the deeper things of the Word of God seeking to equip the Saints for the work of ministry. Their ministry is known worldwide.